MW01229175

LIVELIHOOD AND URBAN POVERTY REDUCTION IN ETHIOPIA: PERSPECTIVES FROM SMALL AND BIG TOWNS

Tegegne Gebre-Egziabher

Organisation for Social Science Research
in Eastern and Southern Africa (OSSREA)

Published in Ethiopia

ISBN: 978-99944-55 -52-2

Organisation for Social Science Research in
Eastern and Southern Africa (OSSREA)
P.O. Box 31971
Addis Ababa, Ethiopia
E-mail: ossrea@ethionet.et
Web site: http//www.ossrea.net

OSSREA acknowledges the support of the Swedish International Development Co-operation Agency (Sida/SAREC), Norwegian Agency for Development Co-operation (NORAD), and The Netherlands' Ministry of Foreign Affairs.

Table of Contents

List of Abbreviations

A.A	Addis Ababa
ADLI	Agricultural Development Led Industrialization
ANOVA	Analysis of Variance
BMCA	Bahir Dar Metropolitan City Administration
BPR	Business Processing Re-engineering
CBO	Community Based Organizations
CSA	Central Statistical Authority
D.D	Dire Dawa
EB	Ethiopian Birr
EEA	Ethiopian Economic Association
EFY	Ethiopian Fiscal Year
FDRE	Federal Democratic Republic of Ethiopia
FUPI	Federal Urban Planning Institute
HICE	Household Income and Consumption Expenditure
IDP	Integrated Development Programme
IHDP	Integrated Housing Development Programme
ILO	International Labour Organization
MDG	Millennium Development Goal
MoFED	Ministry of Finance and Economic Development
MoWR	Ministry of Water Resources
MSE	Micro and Small Enterprises
MUWD	Ministry of Works and Urban Development
NCBP	National Capacity Building Programme
NGO	Non-Governmental Organizations
OECD	Organization for Economic Co-operation and Development
PASDEP	Plan for Accelerated and Sustainable Development to End Poverty
PIPs	Policies, Institutions and Processes
PRSP	Poverty Reduction Strategy Papers

SDPRP	Sustainable Development and Poverty Reduction Programme
SL	Sustainable Livelihood
TVET	Technical and Vocational Education Training
UNDP	United Nations Development Programme
UNCHS	United Nations Center for Human Settlement
UMP	Urban Management Programme
USD	United States Dollar
WMS	Welfare Monitoring Survey

ACKNOWLEDGEMENT

This research was funded by the Organization for Social Sciences Research in Eastern and Southern Africa (OSSREA) under the organization's Senior Scholars Research Grant Programme. The author expresses his deepest gratitude to OSSREA for funding the research.

ABSTRACT

In Ethiopia urban poverty, in comparison to rural poverty and national level poverty, has increased over time. This has necessitated urban poverty reduction as an important area of intervention in urban development and planning. Urban poverty reduction policies and strategies, however, have to be based on needs, capabilities and activities of the urban poor for effective achievements. Policies also need to address the differential situations the poor face in different cities and towns.

The objective of this study is to understand the livelihood situations of the poor in big and small towns, and identify the gaps and linkages between the livelihood requirements of the poor and policies at municipal level. The study was conducted in nine cities and towns of the country, including the capital city. Four of the towns were small towns and five were big or intermediate towns. One poor community was selected from each town as the study area, and a total of five hundred households were randomly selected from all poor communities. A household questionnaire detailing the livelihood of the poor was administered to each participant. A Focus Group Discussion (FGD) was conducted in each community to supplement household level data on different aspects of livelihood. Information was also collected from key informants at municipality and *kebele* levels regarding policy mix, their achievements and effectiveness. In this study a livelihood framework was used to understand the strategies, assets and activities of the poor.

The study findings indicate that in general the poor are asset-less, although there are some differences and similarities regarding asset possession across towns. Those in the small towns are better endowed with livestock resource and house asset but less endowed with quality of labour force. Asset status common to households in the different groups of towns are labour force availability and neighbourhood associations. Lack of financial assets for all households in different towns was also found to be a common characteristic.

In terms of livelihood, casual/piece work was the dominant form of productive activity for most of the households. This is followed by self business in big towns and by wage employment in the capital city. For those engaged in self business, houses are the main business places indicating the importance of home-based activities. In all towns, businesses are run by owners indicating their lack of capacity to hire workers. Income from the business was low with business showing no signs of prosperity. Gender and education differences were noted along the productive activities though the variations across towns in this regard were minimal. In other words, sources of livelihood across towns were similar. The study finds that social and reproductive activities are carried out side by side with productive activities. These activities are important as they provide support for productive activities and livelihood. Shocks and events are experienced by households. Food shortage, ill health, low income and house eviction were the major shocks faced by households.

The foregoing analysis suggests that the livelihood requirements or interventions to improve household livelihoods include assets building strategies, income-generating activities, vulnerability and coping mechanisms.

In terms of policy, all cities and towns, in light of the national urban development policy, implemented micro and small scale enterprise development, integrated housing programme and provision of the land. These policies and programmes, however, have their own implementation problems. The policies have shown some linkages with the livelihood requirements. In particular, the promotion of small and micro enterprises and the integrated housing programme have the potential of addressing livelihood requirements pertaining to employment and housing needs. On the other hand, a number of pointers indicate that there are gaps between the livelihood requirement and existing policies. These gaps pertain to lack of policies that address the assets of the poor, the vulnerabilities of the poor and the differential status of households in different towns.

As a result, the study notes that policies pertaining to enhancing households' asset, local economic development, home-based activities, causal activities, housing affordability, urban safety nets and overcoming city level institutional capacity should be key areas for policy intervention that address the livelihood of the poor and reduce urban poverty.

CHAPTER 1
INTRODUCTION

1.1 Background

The international development policy agenda is currently dominated by the theme of poverty reduction. The theme has been vigorously pursued by multilateral donors, such as The United Nations Development Programme (UNDP), World Bank, and others. Their assistance has also been tuned to pro-poor policy frameworks. Poverty, however, is understood mainly to be a rural phenomenon. This is based on the fact that rural poverty is widespread and pervasive and affects a large segment of the population since the majority of people in less developed countries reside in rural areas. There is, however, an increasing trend of urban growth and with it urban poverty all over the world. Urban growth has brought a host of problem, including unemployment and underemployment, a burgeoning informal sector, deteriorating infrastructure and services, overcrowding, environmental degradation and acute housing shortage (Maxwell 2000). Many national studies and studies of particular urban centres show that one-third to one-half of the nation's urban population or a city's population has incomes too low to allow them to meet basic needs while in many poor African, Asian and Latin American countries, the urban population below poverty line goes to above half of the population (Weglin 1999). It is projected that by the year 2025, about two-third of the world population will live in urban areas and by that time poverty will become a predominant urban problem (*ibid.*). Scholars have coined the term urbanization of poverty to describe the situation.

Urban poverty differs from rural poverty in terms of incidence, economics, demography and politics. The analysis, formulation and implementation of policies should thus be differentiated although policy coordination is obviously needed. Wage labour or the labour market is the main determinant of urban poverty (De Haan 1997). Most of the urban poor earn income from the informal sector. While their earnings do not have as large a seasonal component as those of the rural poor, they are probably almost as unstable because they have little protection from sickness and injury and the unpredictable demand for their services. The poor possess little human capital and almost no physical capital that can be sold or consumed at the time of a sudden dip in their earnings. The poor, having no asset that can be used as collateral, also lack access to credit markets (Mills and Perenia 1994).

Other dimensions of urban poverty include poor environmental conditions that threaten health, changes in prices of basic goods, lack of social network, violence and insecure tenurial status (De Haan 1997; Wratten 1995).

Wratten (*ibid.*) adds commodisation of urban economy, the negative effects of government policies and actions of government polices to the list of urban poverty dimensions. In terms of commodisation, the urban economy is more commercialized than the rural economies and this affects the lives of the urban poor by affecting their needs for subsistence, housing, education, etc. Increases in prices of food, house rent and education fees will put pressure on the urban poor.

The urban poor are affected negatively by the state policies related to security of land. Land policies make the poor to live in an increasing terror of losing their only assets and personal possession. Insecure tenure forces the urban poor to live in self-built, usually illegal housing which is not provided with government services such as schools, health services and the like.

Various factors are put forward as possible causes of urban poverty. Some emphasize macro economic factors emanating from globalization and liberalization. In particular Structural Adjustment Programme, which in many cases resulted in job losses, is viewed as causing the emergence of the new poor (Weglin 1999). This is exacerbated by the weak economic base of many developing countries which has witnessed limited investment and employment. While macro factors may have their own contributions they are not, however, adequate to explain the impoverishment of individuals, families or social groups in a particular country. Micro factors need to be considered in order to have an adequate understanding of poverty well. For instance, the loss of livelihood sources, sudden shocks, changes in family cycle, etc. can generate considerable poverty (*ibid.*).

As the causes of urban poverty could be both macro and micro, the interventions needed to reduce urban poverty should also be envisaged at different levels. The most conventional ones are the macro and the micro interventions. At national or macro level, poverty reduction strategies involve policy and programme interventions which include investment, subsidy, pricing, credit policies and programmes. These poverty reduction strategies have been increasingly reflected in structural adjustment programmes and of late, the Poverty Reduction Strategy Papers or PRSPs. Under structural adjustment programmes, improving productivity is seen as the major objective of reducing poverty. The recent generations of poverty reduction strategies focus on various measures that help reduce poverty.

While the macro level interventions and strategies focus on broad sectoral, cross-cutting and institutional issues, the micro level strategies involve working directly with the community. The interventions are those which support the community activities such as credit, basic infrastructure upgrading, slum upgrading, micro-enterprise development, strengthening community participation, etc. (Vanderschueren *et al.* 1996). Micro level strategies are usually those which are carried out by NGOs, CBOs, etc.

The third layer of interventions are the meso-level interventions that are undertaken by municipalities or local governments and other local development authorities. As the understanding of poverty widens to include poor quality or insecure housing, inadequate services (water, sanitation, health care, access to education), lack of civil and political rights, protection from discrimination and economic shocks, crime and violence, the current or potential role of local governments to contribute to poverty reduction becomes very significant. The meso level forges a link to the macro and micro level. With regard to the macro level, it helps to translate the macro policies to local policies and with regard to the micro level, it provides support to local initiatives at the community level. Municipalities are strategically located to work with the private sector, the NGOs and CBOs in alleviating poverty. In addition, the current world wide trend of decentralization emphasizes the importance of the municipal level to develop an urban poverty reduction strategy since under decentralization many of the responsibilities for social policy are shifted to the local authorities (Wegelin and Borgman 1995). The actions of municipalities, however, have to be based on the needs of the poor and the strategies followed by them. This ensures a viable poverty eradication measure.

In the foregoing, besides highlighting the nature of urban poverty, its causes and intervention, there is an indication of the gravity of urban poverty in general. The gravity of urban poverty varies at country level and in Ethiopia the problem has been on the rise. According to a recently completed poverty profile study, the level of urban poverty has jumped from 33 per cent in 1995/96 to 37 per cent in 1999/2000 and attained a modest decline and reached 35 per cent in 2004/05. This shows a percentage increase of 6 per cent between 1995/96 and 2004/05. This is in contrast to a persistent decline of poverty at national level and in rural areas. At national level, poverty stood at 45 per cent in 1995/96, 44 per cent in 1999/00 and 39 per cent in 2004/05. In rural areas, the level of poverty was 47 per cent in 1995/96, 45 per cent in 1999/00 and 39 per cent in 2004/05 (MoFED 2008).

1.2 Statement of the Problem

With increasing natural population growth and rural urban migration, urbanization has increased in Ethiopia and simultaneously urban poverty has been on the rise. Despite such alarming trend and levels of urban poverty, the focus on the same is very limited. The Ethiopian government has espoused Agricultural Development-Led Industrialization (ADLI) as the development strategy that focuses on enhancing agricultural productivity and thereby bringing about rural development. As a result, rural poverty has been the main preoccupation of government and donor agencies. Various causes of poverty, such as drought, failure of rain, etc. that are directly associated with the lives of the rural people have been the subject of intense attention and concentration. In addition to this, the government has shown less interest in the process of urbanization and urban sector as a development agenda in the country for a long period of time. It is only in the latest PRSP document, namely a Plan for Accelerated and Sustained Development to End Poverty (PASDEP) that urban issues figured following the urban development policy of 2005.

The issue of urban poverty, however, merits a high place on the development agenda of the country mainly because of its increasing trend, the inability of urban centres to address the problem and the need to design appropriate strategies. Policies and strategies, however, have to be based on the needs, capabilities and activities of the urban poor for effective reduction of poverty. In other words, urban poverty reduction has to be tailored to the livelihood aspirations of the poor. This ensures a micro-macro linkage and bases poverty reduction strategies on micro level reality of the poor. In addition, appreciation of urban poverty and devising intervention strategies for the same have to be context specific since the poor face different opportunities and constraints in different places.

A cursory look at the scant urban poverty literature in Ethiopia shows that there are different dimensions of urban poverty that merit further analysis and study. As far as poverty studies in Ethiopia are concerned, first, most studies in Ethiopia have focused on income/consumption measures of urban poverty neglecting the non-income dimensions or livelihood aspects of the poor. This is reflected in poverty studies of Tesfaye (2006), Mekonen (1999), and Mekonen (1996). A few studies, represented by Dessalegn and Aklilu (2002) conducted for ILO, the Community Study of Ellis and Tassew (2005), revolve around unravelling the different dimensions of the poor people's livelihood. These studies show gaps in terms of not adequately capturing the complexities of livelihood at household level. All the studies mentioned above do not relate municipal actions to livelihood requirements and are confined to major or secondary cities. They do not indicate the situation faced by the urban poor in small urban centres. This study attempts to contribute to the literature by examining urban poverty in both small and big urban centres by focusing on the livelihood of the poor households and on the city level policies and institutions to alleviate poverty.

1.3 Objectives

The overall objective of this study is to understand urban poverty in small and big urban centres by focusing on the linkages and gaps between the livelihood of the poor and policies at municipal level.

The specific objectives are:

1. To examine the livelihoods of the urban poor in small and big urban centres by focusing on their assets and activities;

2. To identify urban poverty reduction strategies and institutions at meso (municipal) level;

3. To assess the linkages and gaps between the livelihood requirements of the poor and urban poverty reduction strategies at municipal level; and

4. To suggest strategies that may overcome weaknesses and gaps in mediating the micro and meso perspectives of poverty alleviation.

1.4 Research Questions

The following research questions are put forward to guide the research

1. What is the nature of livelihoods of the urban poor and how does it differ between small and big urban centres?

2. What government sponsored urban poverty reduction strategies are there at municipal levels?

3. What linkages and gaps can be identified between urban poverty reduction strategies and livelihood requirements of the urban poor?

1.5. Research Methods

1.5.1 Sampling Method

The main purpose of the study is to understand the realities pertaining to poor urban households in terms of assets they possess and what they do to make a living using their assets and the problems and opportunities they face in doing so. In addition, it is the purpose of this study to understand the institutional capacities and programmes to alleviate poverty at city (town) level. Households are the final units of analysis for livelihood study and institutions (*kebeles*, city (sub city) municipalities) are the units of analysis for understanding the policies and institutions.

The selection of households involved a multi stage processes. First, the study was conducted in three regions, namely Addis Ababa, Amhara, and Oromiya. These regions were selected because they constitute the highest number of urban population. According to the recent Central Statistics Agency (CSA) census (CSA 2007), Oromiya had 3.4 million urban population, Addis Ababa had 2.8 million, and Amhara had 2.1 million. In total, they constituted 8.3 million or 66.4 per cent of the total urban population in the country. Second, within each region two big and two small urban centres were selected purposively. The regional capital and one intermediate urban centres form the two big urban centres while two small towns found relatively far from the capital city were part of the small towns sample. The purpose of selecting small towns far from the capital city was to minimize the influence bigger towns may have on the livelihood of the small towns' poor. Third, within each town one poor community was selected purposively while in Addis Abeba two sites were selected due to the huge number of the urban population in the city (Table 1.1). The selection of the poor community was made with the help of the City Administrations and Municipalities. In total, ten poor communities were selected in the three regions. The selection of poor communities in each town helped to focus on the poor residents and find adequate evidence of urban poverty. Fourth, households were randomly selected from a list of households in the selected poor communities. The list of households was taken from *kebele*[1] offices. As far as sample size is concerned, the total sample size was 500 households. Since a proportional sample size will not generate statistically reliable size of households as the small towns will be allocated a small proportion, a fixed amount of 50 households were selected from each of the study community. The sample size allows investigations that help to see differences (mean and other differences) between small and big towns and among different towns.

Table 1.1 Distribution of study *kebeles* in each study city/town

City/Town	Selected study *kebele*
Jimma	Mentina
Dessie	*Kebele* 03
Adama	*Kebele* 06/07/08
Bahir Dar	*Kebele* 12 (Gish Abay *kebele*)
Addis Ababa	*Kebele* 13/15 and *Kebele* 14/21
Merawi	*Kebele* 01
Wuchale	*Kebele* 01
Welechiti	*Kebele* 01
Asendabo	*Kebele* 02

SOURCE: Own survey

1.5.2 Data Collection

Type of Data

The information collected was pertaining to assets, sources of vulnerability, and policies and institutions.

Data Collection Techniques

Both qualitative and quantitative data collection methods were used to gather the information:

1. Household survey: Household survey was employed to collect information on the nature of household assets, livelihood strategies, nature of shocks and stresses, responses and livelihood strategies and livelihood outcomes. This was done using a structured questionnaire which was pilot tested initially. The questionnaires were filled in a face to face manner by enumerators and supervisors;

2. Focus Group: Focus group discussions were organized around specific topics such as perception of poverty, assets, livelihood strategies and government assistance. In each study sites two focus

groups, one for women and one for men, were conducted. Each focus group constituted 6-8 members;

3. Unstructured interview: Unstructured interviews, with the help of checklists, were conducted with City Administrations (or Sub-City Administration), municipalities, *kebeles* and city agencies regarding city policies and programmes of poverty alleviation and the institutional arrangement; and

4. Secondary information: Secondary information pertaining to relevant policies and programmes at city level or country level were collected from various ministries and offices at national, regional and city level. Specific studies made in urban poverty in general and urban poverty in the selected cities were also consulted to learn the overall context of the problem.

1.5.3 Data Analysis

Data were descriptively analyzed, making use of descriptive statistics on key variables. Cross-tabulations to assess relationship in few variables were also used. In addition, differences among towns in the various components of livelihood were tested using statistical analysis, such as mean differences, ANOVA, etc. The qualitative data were analyzed by using quotes from the group discussion and summarizing the essence of the discussion.

1.6 Significance of the Study

The study has both academic and policy significance. The study, by shedding light on the livelihood of urban households in both big and small urban centres, helps fill the gap in the urban poverty literature of Ethiopia. . It also throws light on the linkage and relationship between the meso level strategy and the livelihood requirements of the poor. In terms of policy, the study by identifying the opportunities and constraints of the urban poor, provides inputs to generate sound strategies for poverty reduction in Ethiopia.

CHAPTER 2

REVIEW OF RELATED LITERATURE

2.1 Introduction

The literature review focuses on relevant issues needed to understand urban poverty and livelihood. Sections 2.1 and 2.2 view the place of poverty in development discourse and the different conceptualization of poverty. Section 2.3 highlights the nature of urban poverty by focusing on its characteristics. Sections 2.4.1 and 2.4.2 discuss the essentials of livelihood as a tool to understand poverty in general and urban poverty in particular. Section 2.5 surveys urban poverty reduction strategies and policies that focus on different dimensions. Section 2.6 makes a note that small and big towns show different levels of poverty. Section 2.7 examines urban poverty in Ethiopia and shows that there is a gap in addressing poverty. The last section is a conclusion to distil the main lessons of the literature.

2.2 Poverty in Development Thinking

The concern for poverty and poverty reduction has waxed and waned following the orientation of development thinking. In modernization thinking of the 1950s and 1960s, economic growth was accorded a central focus. Economic improvement is assumed to trickle down to the poor. Therefore direct poverty reduction and intervention to improve the living conditions of the poor were not considered to be important (Elbers 2002).

The persistence of poverty and inequality, however, even in the middle of economic growth, led to a shift in development thinking. The redistribution with growth approach and the basic needs approach represent the development thinking of the 1970s. Both approaches recognize the need for poverty reduction through provisions of the basic need and redistribution of growth. In both approaches, the state was given the central role in economic management and planning.

The market oriented development paradigm was dominant in the 1980s. The poor performance of the developing countries was attributed to extended public sector. The argument is that the bloated government and its unproductive expenditure drain the meagre resource and thereby hamper economic development (Tegegne and Asfaw 2002). Governments were accused of performing functions which could have been better undertaken by the private sectors and markets were distorted by too many regulatory policies (Elbers 2002).

Unfettered market was considered a panacea to development problems. The period saw macro-economic reforms such as structural adjustment and liberalization as key strategies of enhancing efficiency and bringing development. The adjustment programmes, however, did not result in the intended outcome. For example, in Sub-Saharn Africa, Klassen (2002) mentioned that SAPs have had only a small impact on poverty despite their initial claim that they would reduce poverty. As the economic benefits and outcomes of the adjustment programmes came to be disappointing, there was a shift in development thinking to the one that provides attention to direct poverty reduction. Towards the end of 1980s and the period of 1990s, the one-sided market oriented development was criticized and a consensus was reached that both the state and the market play a role in development. The consensus was described as follows by Schulpen and Gibbon (2002,2):

> In essence the complementary role of the state and the private sector means that the latter ensures economic growth while the former ensures that the private sector is able to fulfil its role and at the same time makes sure that growth contributes to poverty reduction, does not contribute to environmental degradation and pays attention to gender.

At this juncture, it is important to understand that economic growth is not automatically beneficial to the poor. Growth that benefits the poor must be fostered in order to tackle poverty. This led to the thinking of pro-poor growth which means growth that leads to significant poverty reduction (Klasen 2002). In the words of Kakawni and Son (2006,1):

> An emerging consensus is that growth alone is rather a blunt tool for poverty reduction. To achieve a rapid reduction in poverty, policies of redistribution of income and assets, providing equal access to opportunities for work and employment, social services and benefits need to be emphasized.

Two important ways by which growth could be made pro-poor are first by focusing on those sectors and regions where growth matters for the poor and second by working on public distribution policies (Klassen 2002). Regarding the first, growth must focus on rural areas, must improve income in agriculture and rural non-farm activities and must make intensive use of labour and land which the poor possess. In addition, it should focus on geographic areas of deep poverty. Regarding the second, public redistributive policies, such as transfers and other government, spending are also believed to bring pro-poor growth though there is a need to make caution that too great reliance on these measures may lead to poverty trap and dependency syndrome (*ibid.*).

2.3 The Conceptualization of Poverty

Poverty is conceptualized in a number of ways. It is conceptualized as absolute and relative deprivation. Absolute deprivation or poverty is understood in terms of economic deprivation and that people need to consume a minimum level of goods and services (Beard 2001). Income and consumption are used as measures of absolute poverty. Income poverty measurement assumes that there is a well defined level of standard of living called the 'poverty line" below which a person is deemed to be poor (MoFED 2008). This is set in terms of basic needs. Since having adequate food is the core of basic needs, minimum caloric requirement is used to represent basic needs. Direct caloric intake, food energy intake, and cost of basic needs are the three methods of setting poverty line that uses caloric requirement (MoFED 2008).

The relative deprivation approach defines poverty in relation to either average levels or societal norms. In other words, it refers to consumption equal to a proportion of total or average consumption. The approach is developed in the context of developed country and it attempts to relate the definition of poverty to its potential causes such as economic exploitation and problems of social marginality (Townsend cited in Amis and Rakodi 1994). It is believed that poverty measured with respect to some average is difficult to eradicate.

Conventional poverty line is widely used because it is accepted that inadequate command over commodities is the most important dimension of poverty and a key determinant of other aspects of welfare such as health, longevity and self-esteem (Lipton and Ravallion 1995). It also provides a suitable indicator for making comparisons in time and space (Rakodi 2002a). It enables to measure the numbers and the proportion of poor people over time and among countries and as well as the depth and severity of poverty (OECD 2001). Most common indicators for international comparisons are US$1 a day for low income countries, US$2 for middle income countries, and US$4 for transitional countries (*ibid.*). Many countries establish their own poverty line considering the minimum acceptable in the country.

There are, however, several criticisms directed at income/consumption poverty line measures. Rakodi (2002a) highlights several problems of the poverty line analysis. Among these are that first, it is difficult to estimate consumption in economies partly monetized. Second, it is difficult to include levels of access to publicly supplied goods and common pool resources which could be important components of welfare. Third, there is little evidence on the reliable energy requirement of different groups of people. Fourth, non-food necessities vary between countries, sub-national areas, socio -cultural groups, households and individuals. Fifth, poverty line analysis neglects the dynamics of poverty and fails to distinguish between transient and persistent poverty.

The concept of poverty has broadened since 1990. The World Development report of 1990 supplements a consumption-based poverty measure with others such as nutrition, life expectancy, under-five mortality and school enrolment rates (World Bank 1990a). The broadening of poverty mainly refers to social indicators that reflect well being but not captured in conventional measures of poverty. Along this line, the UNDP defined poverty in terms of human development and introduced the Human

Development Index and Human Poverty Index (Kanbur and Squire 1999). The human poverty index concentrates on three aspects of human deprivation: longevity, literacy, and living standard. Longevity is measured by the percentage of people who die before the age of 40, literacy is measured by the percentage of adults who are literate, and living standard is measured by a combination of the percentage of the population with access to health services, the percentage of population with access to safe water, and the percentage of malnourished children under five (*ibid.*). Beyond these composite measures, poverty can be measured in a disaggregated way in its various dimensions. Economic, human, socio-cultural, political and protective are the different dimensions of poverty (OECD 2001). The economic dimension includes consumption, income, and assets while the human dimension includes health, education and nutrition. The socio-cultural dimension is comprised of status and dignity while the political dimension refers to rights, influence and freedom. The protective elements are related to security and vulnerability. The disaggregated measures are closer to local community and can be used in detailed planning and monitoring (*ibid.*).

The other extension in the conceptualization of poverty is consultation with the poor which attempts to capture the perception and definition of poverty by the poor themselves and how the poor assess their own poverty. This is designated as participatory poverty assessment.

Two main lessons that resulted from participatory poverty assessment are the risk and volatility of income often described as vulnerability and lack of political power or powerlessness of the poor (Kanbur and Squire 1999). Regarding vulnerability, the poor describe how fluctuations, seasons and crisis affect their well being (Elbers 2002). This illuminates the idea that poverty is not only a state of having little but also of being vulnerable to loosing the little one has (*ibid.*). Chambers (1995) mentions that vulnerability has two sides: the external side of exposure to shocks, stress and risks and the internal side of defenceless and a lack of means to cope without damaging loss. The poor are powerless, because it is difficult for them to organize and bargain as they are mainly preoccupied with access to resources and income (*ibid.*). They are also easy to ignore and exploit. Other notions added to the concept of poverty include deprivation, entitlement and social exclusion.

2.4 Urban Poverty

In absolute terms, rural poverty is more widespread than urban poverty in the third world countries. This has prompted many international agencies to exhibit a particular bias towards the rural poor (Beall 1997). Such biases are difficult to contest. However, it is increasingly becoming true that urban poverty is showing an increasing trend. The 2006/07 state of the world cities report predict that for the first time in the world history, the majority of human beings will live in cities by the year 2007 (UN-Habitat 2007). At the same time the year will also mark that the number of slum dwellers in the world will cross the one billion mark (*ibid.*). Urban poverty and inequality will characterize many cities with urban growth becoming synonymous with slum formation in some regions (*ibid.*).

Despite this, however, there is a tendency to underestimate urban poverty. Satterthwaite (1997) mentioned that international statistics underestimates the proportion of urban poor. For instance in 1988, the world Bank report stated that only 330 million poor people live in urban areas in the third world implying that more than three-quarter of the population of the third world were not poor in 1988. Such estimates were found out to be in disagreement with that of the national estimates which in many cases indicated that more than half of the urban population is below the poverty line. Satterthwaite (1997) argues that even national statistics undermine the proportion of urban households living in poverty mainly due to the use of low national poverty line set for both rural and urban areas. This places many urban poor above the poverty line while in actual fact they lack the income they need to cover the costs of basic necessities-safe drinking water, adequate quality housing with piped water, adequate sanitation, health-care and children's education (*ibid.*).

In order to understand the nature of urban poverty, there is a need to understand its characteristics. Satterthwaite (2001) argues that urban poverty exhibits eight major characteristics. These are: 1) inadequate income; 2) inadequate, unstable or risky asset base; 3) inadequate shelter; 4) inadequate provision of public infrastructure; 5) inadequate provision of basic services; 6) limited or no safety nets; 7) inadequate protection; and 8) voicelessness or powerlessness. All these features result in inadequate consumption, overcrowded, insecure and unhygienic shelter, vulnerability and lack of entitlements.

Beall and Fox (2006) identified ten issues to characterize urban poverty (Box 1). These characteristics reveal the dimensions which differentiate urban poverty from rural poverty.

Box 1: Characteristics of urban poverty and vulnerability

- Reliance on monetized economy
- Reliance on the informal economy
- Inadequate housing
- Insecurity of tenure
- Lack of access to basic services
- Vulnerability to diseases
- Environmental hazards
- Social fragmentation
- Exposure to violence and crime
- Increasing experience of warfare and terrorism

SOURCE: Beall and Fox (2006), p. 7

Reliance on Monetized and Informal Economy

In urban setting, people rely on market exchanges to obtain basic necessities such as food, shelter, water and electricity. They need higher level of income than rural households to avoid poverty. Cash income is needed to pay for public transport, schools, housing, water, food, health care, child care, etc.. The costs of all these services are higher in urban areas and form significant parts of the poor's expenditure. For example food is expensive for urban households who have no possibility of growing food or raising livestock. In terms of housing, it is believed that many tenant households spend more than a third of their income on rent (Satterhwaite and Tacoli 2002). Similarly, for many households the payments made to water vendors often form 10 per cent and even 20 per cent of the household income (*ibid.*).

The primary source of income to pay for these necessities is wage labour. As a result, the labour market forms an important determinant of poverty. A range of issues concerning the labour market affect the conditions of the poor. Labour market regulations and legislations influence minimum wage, hiring and firing, employment protection, etc. These can have counterproductive effects on the poor affecting the cost of labour and constraining job opportunities (World Bank 1990a). The kind of jobs people engage also have implication for urban poverty. For example, people with stable jobs are less likely to be poorer than people who have an unstable casual job (de Haan 1997).

The labour market is influenced by economic restructuring. For example, critics of globalization believe liberalization and international competition and internal liberalization lead to higher unemployment, excessive casualisation of labour markets, economic instability and deteriorating living conditions (Gilbert 1997).

An important aspect of labour market that influences poverty is the informal economy. The poor tend to engage heavily in the informal economy. Rogerson (1996) distinguishes between two types of informal enterprises: the survivalist and the micro-enterprises. The former represents sets of activities undertaken by people unable to get wage employment and formal employment. The income from these sources falls short of the minimum level of income. Poverty and desperate attempt to survive are typical features of these enterprises. The micro-enterprises are small businesses often involving the owner and some family members. These businesses lack the elements of formality and have very limited capital base. Owners often are without the required skills.

Inadequate Housing and Insecure Tenure

A large proportion of the urban dwellers live in substandard housing and informal settlements. For example in India, Ghana, Cambodia and Bolivia more than 50 per cent of all urban residents live in informal settlements (Beall and Fox 2006). Houses in these settlements are makeshift shelters of bricks and zinc sheets, scavenged pieces of wood and industrial scraps (*ibid*). These houses are not only overcrowded and unhygienic but are also not connected to the formal structures such as drainage and sewage systems. In Addis Ababa, it is less than 3 per cent of the houses which are connected to sewage systems. The current sewer system in the city is a small system designed to serve 200,000 people, and often it is not in full capacity working conditions (Dierig 1999). At its best, the modern sewerage system serves only 0.3 per cent of the housing units and only 2 per cent of the city's population (*ibid.*).

Imbalance between the supply and demand of housing in cities results in illegal settlements. This happens usually as the formal housing market and government policies cannot match the pace of urban growth. Market forces and government restrictive regulations often cause high land cost which poses difficulty for the large majority of the people and especially for the poor to access land in cities. As a result, non-formal occupation of land or informal tenure emerges. This is now the largest and fast growing form of tenure in urban areas representing between 15 and 70 per cent of total urban population (Durand-Lasserve cited in Payne 2002). Informal settlements or sometimes called as squatter units have no legal titles or legally binding rental/lease agreements. This exposes households to the threats of eviction and confrontation or abuse by landowners or officials. Eviction and the threats of eviction often characterize the lives of the poor in urban areas. For example across Africa, 4 million people were evicted from their homes in 2001-02 and millions more continue to live with the threat of eviction (Beall and Fox 2006). People squatting on illegal land often occupy land that exposes them to environmental risks such as steep slopes in ravines, river banks, or areas susceptible to land slides or pollution (Payne 2002).

Lack of Access to Basic Services

The poor in urban areas suffer from lack of access to basic services. Adequate access to health, education, water, sewage, including well serviced houses is a constraint faced by the urban poor. Though it is believed that urban dwellers have better access than rural dwellers, the poor in cities pay high cost for such services. For example, residents in Nairobi living in under-serviced areas pay up to 11 times more for water sold by private vendors than those who have access to piped water while in Dhaka the figure is close to 25 times more (Beall and Fox 2006). In Addis Ababa, the charge for water from public water taps amounts 10 cents per 60 litter while households with own connections pay 0.5 cents per 100 litters. This rate is a subsidized rate and there is no full cost recovery. A cost recovery scheme will definitely raise the charges. Private water vendors in the city charge 10 to 50 cents per 20 litters (Diereg 1999). The existing water charges favour middle and high income people with own connections who pay subsidized rates while the poor depending on water vendors are disadvantaged by paying higher charges.

The lack of basic services brings enormous health burden and this seems to be unnoticed by many definitions of poverty (Satterthwaite 1997). Hundreds of millions of urban dwellers in the South who are believed to have incomes above the poverty line live in a very poor quality housing, often overcrowded with a great lack of infrastructure and services (*ibid.*). Nearly two decades ago, it is estimated that about 600 million people urban dwellers in Africa, Asia and Latin America live in 'life and health threatening homes and neighbourhoods because of poor housing, inadequate provision of water, sanitation, drainage, garbage collection and health care (*ibid.*).

Vulnerability to Diseases and Environmental Hazards

The poor in urban areas live in appalling environmental conditions. Poor households, because of their low income, are forced to live in cheap, high density, environmentally poor and physically dangerous locations near industrial facilities, toxic waste, solid waste pumps, railway lines, etc. (Meikle 2002). As a result, they suffer from numerous diseases such as typhoid, cholera, malaria, diarrheal diseases, intestinal worms, etc. which are all associated with poor environmental condition (*ibid.*).

Social Fragmentation

In general, cities are culturally diverse and socially more fragmented than rural areas (Meikle 2002). As a result, community and kinship ties are loose. This threatens the traditional forms of managing health risks, economic insecurity and tensions (Beall and Fox 2006). Under such circumstances, families struck by illness or natural disasters may find themselves selling the assets they have, scavenging in the streets and even engaging in criminal activities (*ibid.*). Social disintegration and community breakdown in cities could worsen the conditions of the poor in urban areas and increase their vulnerability.

An opposing view to the conditions of social fragmentation in urban areas is the realization that a key asset for both the urban and the rural poor is social capital which includes social relations among individuals in urban areas and even between rural and urban households (Meikle 2002). The latter is an example of social capital transcending the city to include wider rural-urban linkages (Tacoli 1999). Social capital is believed to be a critical resource which contributes to the wellbeing of the poor. The livelihood framework considers social capital as one form of assets possessed by the poor.

Exposure to Violence, Crime, War and Terrorism

It has been increasingly recognized that crime and violence are major development problems in urban areas (UN-Habitat 2002). The incidence of crime and violence is found out to be high among cities. A survey conducted in 2001 in Nairobi city revealed that 37 per cent of Nairobi's residents had been victims of robbery, 22 per cent a victim of theft and 18 per cent had been personally assaulted during the year preceding the survey (*ibid.*). The same survey also showed that 29 per cent of all homes and 30 per cent of all commercial enterprises had fallen victim to burglary and 23 per cent of all those who had either household or farm equipment on their property experienced a theft (*ibid.*). Similarly, Beall and Fox (2006) noted that there is a rise in urban crime across the developing world and Eastern Europe.

Societal and individual well being as well as country's development will be affected negatively in crime and violence situations. Though crime happens throughout a city, its intensity is higher in informal settlements where the poor live and the poor residents are the main victims of all crime (UN-Habitat 2002). This erodes the assets of the urban poor and increases their vulnerability.

While the above depicts the characteristics of urban poverty, various factors are put forward as possible causes of urban poverty. Some emphasize macro-economic causes emanating from globalization and liberalization. In particular structural adjustment programmes (SAP), which in many cases resulted in job losses, price increase, wage restraints, elimination of food, housing and transport subsidies are viewed as causing poverty (Weglin 1999; Beall 1997). The result of the SAP is the creation of the 'new poor' in urban areas. Mabogunje (2006) distinguished between the 'new poor', the 'borderline poor' and the 'chronic poor'. The 'new poor' comprise retrenched civil servants or employees laid off by public and private enterprises as a direct consequence of structural adjustment while the 'borderline' poor are those unskilled workers in urban industry, whose income are so low that price increase resulting from structural adjustment push them to poverty line. The 'chronic poor' are those who are extremely poor even before the adjustment programme started and their condition perhaps becomes worse because of it.

The weak economic base of many developing countries, limited investment and employment in the face of fast rates of urbanization could also be a prime cause of poverty. In particular, resource deficiencies, poor urban management and absence of effective urban governance all combine to result in inadequate employment and services particularly for those in poverty (Beall 1997). In addition, many forms of deprivation faced by poor households (and non-poor households) are more the result of weak, ineffective unrepresentative or corrupt government than that of income levels (Satterthwaite 1997). This is because though people may have income above poverty line, it is not a guarantee to secure access to safe and sufficient water supplies, sanitation and drainage, or access to schools and health-care service due to the capacity of the public, private or non-profit institutions to ensure provision. This implies that many forms of deprivation associated with poverty can be addressed by more competent and effective public or private institutions.

While macro factors may have their own contribution they are not, however, adequate to explain the impoverishment of individuals, families or social groups in a particular country. Micro factors need to be considered in order to have an adequate understanding of poverty well. For instance, the loss of livelihood sources, sudden shocks, changes in family cycle, etc. can generate considerable poverty (Weglin 1999).

2.5 Livelihood and the Livelihood Framework in Urban Setting

2.5.1 Livelihood Defined

The concept of livelihood is used widely in poverty and rural development literature. A livelihood is the way people earn a living be it in town or in rural areas or both. According to Chambers and Conway (1992,7) a livelihood 'comprises capabilities, assets (stores, resources, claims and access) and activities required for a means of living'. Ellis (2000) criticizes Chambers and Conway for their use of capabilities in the definition since the meaning of capabilities overlaps assets and activities.

In the definition of livelihood, assets refer to five main categories of capitals and these are natural, physical, human, financial and social. Natural capital refers to the natural resources (land, water, trees) that yield products. Physical capital is asset brought into existence by economic production processes. Human capital refers to the education levels and the health status of individuals and population. Financial capital is related to the stock of cash that can be accessed in order to purchase production or consumption goods. Social capital refers to the social networks and association in which people participate and derive support to contribute to their livelihoods. Ellis (2000) modifies the definition provided by Chambers and Conway to emphasize the notion of access in assets. In particular, social relations and institutions that mediate individuals or family's capacity to have access are recognized. Accordingly, it is indicated that:

> A livelihood comprises assets (natural, physical, human, financial, and social capital), the activities and the access to these (mediated by institutions and social relations) that together determine the living gained by the individual or household (Ellis 2000, 10).

The question of access in the livelihood definition is further examined by other authors as well (De Haan and Zoomers 2005; Bebbington 1999). This is elaborated by indicating that access is governed by social relations, institutions, organizations and power (De Haan and Zommers 2005).

Two important concepts which are related to the livelihood analysis are the sustainable livelihood and livelihood diversification. Based on the recognition of the importance of the natural resource base to rural livelihood and the vulnerability that characterizes the position of the poor: "A livelihood is sustainable when it can cope with and recover from stress and shocks and maintain or enhance its capabilities and assets both now and in the future while not undermining the natural resource base" (Carney 1998, 4).

Livelihood diversification has made significant contribution to rural livelihood. This has made policy makers to focus attention on non-agricultural sources of income as well as agriculture. Ellis defines rural livelihood diversification as: "The process by which rural households construct an increasingly diverse portfolio of activities and assets in order to survive and to improve their standard of living" (Ellis 2000,14).

The livelihood approach to poverty is based on the premise that livelihood is fit to capture how the poor live, what their priorities are and what can help them (Chamber 1995). Interest in livelihood rose as a result of a critical response to the inadequacy of an approach to poverty which mainly measures income/consumption and focuses on outcomes. Such an approach undermines poverty processes, the multidimensionality of poverty and the institutional dimensions associated with the solutions (Beall and Kankji 1999). The livelihood approach, on the other hand, looks beyond income and aggregate consumption measures and emphasizes the following elements (Rossietie 2000).

a) Context: The livelihood framework requires the understanding of the social, economic, political environment in which the assets exist. Understanding of resources, technologies, population growth, culture, conflict, climate, markets and understanding of the political and administrative structure of the government and the private sector;

b) Mulitsectoral approach: The framework forces one to think about strategies to enhance and improve livelihoods in holistic and multi-sectoral perspective rather than in a disintegrated and sectoral perspective; and

c) Empowerment: Empowerment is one of the indirect outcomes of the livelihood. The building up of assets increases one's ability to influence the policies and institutions which influence livelihood options.

2.5.2 The Livelihood Framework in Urban Setting[2]

The fact that urban poverty reduction has to address the livelihood aspirations of the poor is a compelling reason for using the sustainable livelihood (SL) approach. The SL approach, as analytical framework, focuses on the assets of the poor and the strategies they employ to make a living. The approach provides a framework to assess resources and assets available to households and how they are linked to strategies to reach desired outcome. According to the framework, households decide to mobilize and allocate their resources (their assets and capabilities). This results in activities (directly income earning activities; coping strategies etc). Income resulting from the activities are allocated among competing demands (consumption, investment, saving) to bring desired outcome which includes basic needs (health, water, education, food, shelter etc). The assets, strategies and outcomes are seen in contexts-the political, economic, social and institutional context in which households are situated. The contexts in turn decrease or increase vulnerability. Vulnerability is also related to resources or assets that an individual or household holds.

The Core of SL Approaches are:

1. **Vulnerability**: This refers to the insecurity or well being of individuals or communities in the face of changing environment. The changes could be in the form of sudden shocks, long term trends or seasonal cycles. The extent of vulnerability relates both to the resilience resisting and recovering from external threats.

2. **Assets**: These refer to the resources on which people draw to carry out their livelihood strategies. The resources include different forms of capital: financial, human, social, physical, natural and political capital. People may not always posses the assets they use. They have different extent of access to and control over these assets. In the SL approach, the issue of access and how access can be improved is significant.

3. **Policies, Institutions and Processes (PIPs):** These are the broad range of social, political, economic and environmental factors determining peoples' choice and shaping livelihoods. They determine access to the various types of assets.

4. **Livelihood Strategies**: These refer to planned activities people undertake to build their livelihoods. Included under livelihood strategies are coping strategies to respond to shocks in short-term and adaptive strategies to improve circumstances in the long term.

5. **Livelihood Outcomes**: These are the results of peoples' livelihood strategies and feed back into the vulnerability context and asset bases. While successful strategies help build asset bases, poor livelihood deplete asset bases and increase vulnerability.

Figure 1 provides the sustainable livelihood framework as developed by DFID and the various interrelationships among the core elements. The SL approach was first developed in rural context. Subsequently, however, it is utilized in the urban context to reduce poverty. The application of the SL approach in urban context, however, has to accommodate the urban features in its core elements. For instance, with regard to vulnerability, the sources in urban setting refer to social context of cities, the nature of the urban economy, the urban environment and urban systems of governance. In terms of assets, income from the sale of labour and access to credit are important financial capital. House is one of the most important assets for poor households because of its shelter and income generating use (Moser 1998). Public infrastructure is also another important physical resource. The role of land and common property resources are less important in urban settings though the poor may use river water and other natural resources.

With regard to livelihood strategies, income enhancing activities in urban areas may include domestic services, urban agriculture, renting out rooms while expenditure reducing may include scavenging, cutting transport cost etc. Other activities such as casual labour, specialized occupation, migration, begging, theft, transporting goods and, processing may be some of the activities common to both urban and rural. The policy, institutions and processes (PIPs) are key concerns in urban areas. In terms of policy, the urban poor depend on the delivery of infrastructure and services by city institutions. The existence of pro-poor policy has implication for building the livelihood of the poor. Institutional relationship between the poor and local and municipal governance has implication for urban poverty. Process such as urbanization will have implication for urban poverty as this may open opportunity for casual labourer particularly in peri-urban areas.

Livelihood and Urban Poverty Reduction in Ethiopia

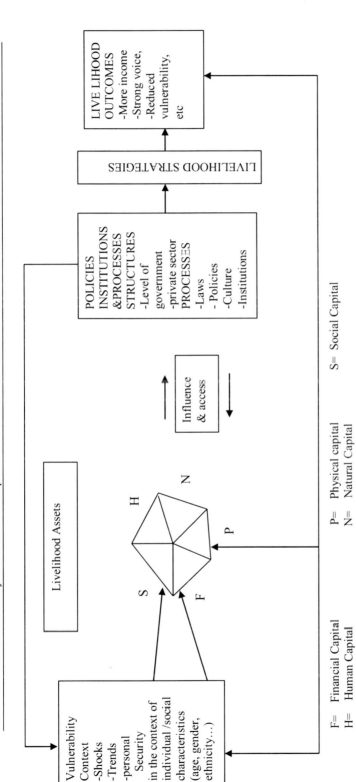

Figure 1. Sustainable Livelihoods Framework

F= Financial Capital   P= Physical capital   S= Social Capital
H= Human Capital   N= Natural Capital

SOURCE: Farrington *et al.* (2002)

2.6 Urban Poverty Reduction Programmes

Poverty alleviation programmes seek to provide immediate palliative in the short term, whilst poverty reduction programmes are systematic approaches which eventually lead to eradication of poverty.

A very useful departure point for poverty reduction programmes is the conceptualization of poverty as multiple deprivation involving lack of income, assets, legal rights, resources or contacts to secure political advantage, access to education, health care, emergency services, adequate housing etc. Such multiple deprivations need multiple programmes at multiple levels.

Beall (1997) identified four broad categories of policy responses to urban poverty. First is the need to tackle poverty at metropolitan level in terms of local economies and within an institution framework. This is necessitated because dysfunctional cities with poor communication system, power system etc do not encourage the productive capacities of the local urban economies which reduce the employment and investment opportunities of the poor. Second, income and consumption poverty exist in cities and it has to be tackled in terms of targeted welfare and relief programmes. Third, the living environment in low income settlement requires appropriate policy response. In this regard security of tenure and occupation, services such as safe water supply and sanitation, affordable transportation of the poor etc are critical to the needs of the poor and have to be properly addressed. Fourth is policy response to address the lack of public safety and the growth of urban violence which reduces the energy of the poor and the cities. One policy focus in this regard is in the area of physical and psycho-social security.

In terms of programmes, Satterthwaite (1997) indicates that there are a range of actions that centre on three areas of interventions: increasing income or assets for low income households, upholding human rights and improving housing and basic services. Table 2.1 gives the details of these ranges of actions.

The World Bank (1990a) identified a number of policy intervention addressing different dimension of urban poverty. These are labour market and employment, land, housing and urban service, financial market, public finance, decentralization and intergovernmental relations, urban governance and capacity building.

Table 2.1 Aspects of poverty reduction

Increasing income and /or assets	
A job through employment creation	Where successful, these bring new jobs and/or enhanced incomes, although external support must understand local constraints on new enterprises being able to generate adequate incomes. There may be considerable potential for linking employment creation for low income groups with public works to improve water supply, provision for sanitation and drainage, improved roads and all weather paths, health care centres or with staffing new or improved services
Credit for small or informal enterprise	Credit for small scale enterprise must respond to women's needs and priorities, as well as men's
Education, literacy and vocational training	In general these should increase income-earning capacity as well as providing other advantages. In many countries, biases against women in education and vocational training will need to be addressed. The barriers to education for low-income households caused by the introduction of school fees or their increase in other education costs (for instance of school uniforms or examination fees) have to be addressed.
Providing squatter with legal tenure	Increased security of tenure for owner occupiers in illegal settlements reduces the risk of eviction, increases the value of their asset and the possibility of obtaining credit.
Emergency credit	The ready availability of emergency credit can greatly reduce the vulnerability of low-income groups to economic shocks
Upholding Human Rights	
Access to justice within the judiciary system	This includes legal systems that protect citizens from forced eviction. It also includes public programmes to reduce crime and violence within the low-income settlements and community programmes to halt the abuse of women and children within families. It is also

	important to establish the rights of low income urban dwellers to land for cultivation and the need to halt the harassment of hawkers
The right to vote, to have representative government and to organize to make demands	Achieving recognition by government agencies of the civil and political rights of low-income urban dwellers and their entitlements to public support, public services and public accountability.
Improved Housing and Basic Services	
Tenure of Housing	Secure tenure generally promotes households investment in improving the house and gives greater capacity to negotiate with local authorities for improved services.
Improved water, sanitation, drainage and garbage collection	If adequately provided, this removes tremendous health burden and also considerably reduces the time needed for domestic tasks. This brings particular advantages to the person in the household who is responsible for collecting water and managing household wastes-usually the women. It is also important in reducing the vulnerability of many low-income settlements to floods and rain induced landslides.
Basic health care	If available, this reduces the economic and health costs of illness and injury. There are particular advantages for the person in the household who takes care of those who are sick or injured (usually the women)
Day care	This increases the time for those who look after young children and also means young children are not left in the care of older siblings. Day care centres also provide regular health checks for infants and young children and monitor their nutritional status; they can also provide stimulus and support for children's physical and mental development. Day care centres are particularly valuable in increasing women's income earning capacities and especially valuable to single parents (usually women heads) households.
Housing finance	Housing credit available to low-income households who want to build, extend or buy their own homes allows them to afford better

	quality housing and if building it themselves, to reduce the time taken to complete it. Credit can also be used to allow improved infrastructure and services for whole settlements- for example piped water and sewers installed with each household able to repay the capital costs over several years.
Transport	Cheap and efficient public transport can greatly reduce the disadvantage for low income households of living in peripheral locations and if city wide could also help reduce the price of housing

SOURCE: Satterthwaite (1997,17-18)

A range of actions can be undertaken at macro, micro and meso levels (Vandershuren *et al.* 1996). The macro level involvement includes policy and programme interventions defined and implemented by the central government which include investment, subsidy, pricing, credit policies and programmes (*ibid.*). The micro level involvement is at the community level in which a variety of activities such as credit, infrastructure upgrading, slum upgrading, micro enterprise development and community participation could be pursued NGOs and CBOs are active at this level. The community initiated approach has the advantage of being cheap and empowering the community to address problems and negotiate with external agencies for resources and support (Satterthwaite 1997).

The meso level is that found between the macro and the micro and in urban areas this corresponds to a municipal level. Key roles at the municipal level are facilitation of community initiatives and overall coordination of provision of urban services (Vandershuren *et al.* 1996). More specifically, the poverty reduction roles of municipalities involve facilitation, coordination, planning and programming, implementation and monitoring of different infrastructure and municipal services such as land management, housing and housing finance, municipal infrastructure and services, micro enterprises and finance, urban agriculture, access to community credit, access to justice, and concerns of vulnerable groups (Wegelin 1999).

Different responsibilities are allocated to urban governments which have important bearing on most important aspects of urban poverty. Many authors agree that there are at least six areas where local governments have a particular important role. These are access to land for housing, the provision of basic infrastructure and services, serving and supporting a prosperous local economy, pro-poor orientation within local economic policies, access to justice and local political system that are inclusive of the poor and the disadvantaged groups (*ibid.*).

Wegelin and Borgman (1995), summarizing UNCHS/UNDP/World Bank urban management programme (UMP) research, identified the following areas about the importance of municipal level in poverty reduction. These are improving regulatory frameworks, access to municipal services, employment creation, protection from crime, and natural disasters and overall coordination and integration. According to Amis (2001), the role accorded to municipalities can be collapsed into three areas: economic growth, public services and improving local environment. Municipalities or local government will have either sole responsibilities or shared responsibilities with higher levels of government or play supervisory or regulatory role for private sector or NGO providers in addressing the above roles. At this juncture it is important to emphasize that the capacity of local government or municipalities to reduce poverty is influenced by the links with higher levels of government. In this regard higher levels of government should ensure that urban government structures are representative of and accountable to citizens and that urban governments have the necessary power and resources to fulfil their responsibilities (*ibid.*).

2.7 Poverty in Small and Big Centres

There is a view that the acuteness and incidence of the various attributes of urban poverty can be expected to vary with the size of a particular urban centre. For example, urban poverty is believed to be more extreme in metropolitan areas than small cities (Mabogunje 2006). In describing one of the reasons for the low estimate of urban poverty in some developing countries, Satterthwaite (1997) pointed out that living costs are assumed to be the same wherever the household lives particularly between rural and urban despite the fact that living costs are higher in urban areas. For example, the costs of building and renting housing, getting to and from work and paying for water will be higher in big urban centres than in small urban centres. The cost of basic necessities is likely to be greatest in the larger or more prosperous cities. The costs of public transport, schools, health-care, housing, basic services, etc are likely to be higher in the larger and more prosperous urban cities than in smaller and or less prosperous urban centres. Similarly, in large urban centres there are fewer opportunities for reducing costs through some subsistence production (e.g. growing food) or through access to free resources (e.g. wood for building or for fuel (Satterthwaite 1997). The high cost of living in big urban centres therefore exacerbates poverty.

In the contrary in India, it was found out that the incidence of poverty declined with the size of towns (Dubey *et al.* 2001). This is attributed to the fact that larger cities provide higher economic and social infrastructure (*ibid.*). While the economic infrastructure affects the poverty incidence through greater income earning potential, the social infrastructure may directly help in reducing poverty by allowing greater access to poverty reducing transfers (*ibid.*).

The difference between small and big urban centres is also studied by Brockerhoff and Brennan (1998) in relation to well being as measured by infant mortality rate. The result showed that cities with over a million population showed a slower decline of infant mortality rate compared to smaller cities or communities (*ibid.*).

The above discussion shows that while there is no conclusive agreement on the direction of the relation between town size and poverty, the results indicate that poverty and well being vary by city size. It, therefore, cannot be assumed that different towns face similar conditions of poverty.

2.8 Urban Poverty in Ethiopia: Nature and Extent

The rapid pace of urbanization (more than 4 per cent) which is not matched by parallel progress and prosperity is a growing concern in Ethiopia. The rapid pace of urbanization is mainly fuelled by rural-urban migration which is generated both by seemingly attractive livelihoods in urban areas as pull factors and rural poverty as push factor. As a result, rural-urban migration seems to transfer poverty from rural to urban areas. The term urbanization of poverty seems to be a best fit for situations in Ethiopia.

The incidence of urban poverty has shown a dramatic increase. It has jumped from 33 per cent in 1995/96 to 37 per cent in 1999/2000 showing an increase of 11 per cent (Table 2.2). It has however shown a modest decline in 2004/05 and reached 35 per cent (MoFED 2008). The 2004/05 poverty line has shown a percentage increase of 5.7 per cent over that of 1995/96. This is in contrast to a constant decline of both total poverty and rural poverty. Total poverty has declined from 45 per cent in 1995/96 to 44 per cent in 1999/00 and 39 per cent in 2004/05. The percentage decline between 1995/96 and 2004/05 is 13.3 per cent. Rural poverty has declined from 47 per cent in 1995/96 to 45 per cent in 1999/00 and 39 per cent in 2004/05. This shows a percentage decline of 17.02 per cent between the years of 1995/96 and 2004/05.

Table 2.2 Trend of poverty in Ethiopia: 1995/96 and 2004/05

	National			Rural			Urban		
Year/period	P0	P1	P2	P0	P1	P2	P0	P1	P2
1995/96	0.455	0.129	0.051	0.475	0.134	0.053	0.332	0.099	0.041
1999/00	0.442	0.119	0.045	0.454	0.122	0.046	0.369	0.101	0.039
2004/05	0.387	0.083	0.027	0.393	0.085	0.027	0.351	0.077	0.026

SOURCE: MoFEd 2008

Similarly, while a significant improvement is recorded in depth (P1) and severity of poverty (P2) at national level and in rural areas, improvements in these indicators in urban areas are much below the national and rural levels (see Table 2.2)

Income distribution in Ethiopia also shows that urban areas depict a larger inequality than rural areas or the whole of the country. A study has shown that consumption inequality measured by Gini coefficient shows a moderate increase at national level, no increase at rural level and a high increase in urban areas (MoFED 2008). The Gini coefficient in urban areas increased from 0.34 to 0. 44 while nationally the increase was only from 0.29 to 0.30 (Table 2.3).

Table 2.3 Trends in inequality as measured by Gini Coefficient of consumption

	National	Rural	Urban
1995/96	0.29	0.27	0.34
1999/00	0.28	0.26	0.38
2004/05	0.30	0.26	0. 44

SOURCE: MoFED (2008)

Signs of urban poverty are clearly visible in many cities of the country. Beggars, shanty homes, malnourished individuals, scattered garbage, etc are visible in many places (EEA 2004/05). In addition, other manifestations such as haphazard spatial organization and poor physical growth, poor educational services, deteriorating urban environment, poor internal access roads and traffic management, poor access to water supply, overcrowded and poor housing, mushrooming slums and squatter houses, poor environment of business operation are noted in many urban centres of the country (Shewaye 2002). What is worse is that with increased urbanization, these different dimensions of urban poverty are likely to increase.

Urban poverty shows a variation among urban centres. Table 2.4 gives the levels and changes of urban poverty in different towns. Though some towns have shown a decline, the major towns such as Addis Abeba, Dire Dawa Harar, Jimma, and Adama have witnessed a significant increase in the levels of urban poverty[3].

Table 2.4 Poverty incidence and changes in poverty incidence in selected towns (percentages)

Major towns	Poverty 1995/96 (%)	Poverty 1999/00 (%)	Poverty 2004/05(%)	Change (%) 1995/96-2004/05
Mekele	46.4	42.8	34. 4	-25.9
Gonder	33.9	17.5	35.3	4.1
Dessie	71.9	31.3	32.7	-54.5
Bahridar	38.2	22.3	29.6	-22.5
Bishoftu	44.2	36.7	31.6	-28.5
Adama	29.0	28.5	30.0	3. 4
Jimma	29.2	37.0	31.6	8.2
Harar	29.1	35.0	32.6	12
AA	30.0	36.2	32.6	8.7
Diredawa	24.6	31.5	32.9	33.7
National urban	33.2	36.9	35.1	5.7
National-total	45.5	44.2	38.7	-14.9

SOURCE: MoFED (2008)

Urban poverty in Ethiopia is fuelled by many factors. Poor agricultural performance with the growing shortage of land leads to massive rural-urban migration. According to an in-depth analysis of the 1994 census and the 1999 labour force survey, the proportion of rural-urban migration forms 23 per cent. The main reason for urban-ward migration was found out to be job search (Golini *et al.* 2001). This implies that rural-urban migrants pose a huge pressure on the urban labour market leading to urban poverty if the job market fails to accommodate the migrants.

Most cities in Ethiopia lack internal dynamism because of their weak economic base (Shewaye 2002). In many cases this is a result of the historical origin of towns. Many towns in Ethiopia originated as political capitals and garrison towns to serve political and military purposes (Akalu 1967). Other towns have mainly employment in civil service, the military or small catering services and do not provide bases for industrialization (Tegegne 2005). Such lack of dynamism means lack of enough production and services support to meet the growing needs of rural-urban migrants, the urban residents and the informal economy. Unemployment is therefore very high in urban Ethiopia. According to a recent labour force survey, the unemployment rate in urban Ethiopia is 20.6 per cent with the highest incidence being among females (27.2 per cent) compared to males (13.7 per cent) (CSA 2006). A feature that is worth taking note of unemployment rate in urban Ethiopia besides its high level is the presence of unemployed skilled labour. The unemployed in Ethiopia include a large section of the educated persons (EEA 2004/05). The recent national labour force survey puts the unemployment rate of literate (7.8 per cent) to be higher than illiterate (3.5 per cent) (CSA 2006). The rate of unemployment is also higher for those who completed general education (28.8 per cent) as opposed to those who have no general education (23.2 per cent) (CSA 2006). The reason for many educated people to be unemployed in many urban areas is due to the fact that those who completed their 12 years of schooling but who fail to pursue their studies become unemployed and also due to the government decision to stop allocating graduates of higher institution to employment (EEA 2004/05). According to some estimate, there are about 190,000 educated unemployed persons in any given year (Abbi 2005). On top of unemployment, under-employment caused by increased casualization of labour is also widespread in urban areas and this leads to unstable household income and increased vulnerability to poverty (*ibid.*). The informal economy is a significant source of livelihood in urban Ethiopia. In 1999, the sector provided employment for a little over half (51 per cent) of the urban work force. Though according to the recent official statistics, this has decreased to about one-quarter (26 per cent), it still provides livelihood for a significant proportion of the urban labour force in some cities such as Dire Dawa (41 per cent), Desse (39 per cent), Jijiga (39 per cent), Gonder (39 per cent) (CSA 2006). Though entry to the sector is quite easy, entrepreneurs in the sector are highly vulnerable for a variety of reasons (Dessalegn and Aklilu 2002).

As in other developing countries, the economic reform programme has its contribution to urban poverty in Ethiopia. The reform in Ethiopia included currency devaluation, privatization and liberalization of the market. This has resulted in price increase, contraction of the labour market and a greater risk of unemployment (Dessalegn and Aklilu 2002). Privatization of state owned enterprises and streamlining of civil servants have led to retrenchment of workers in urban Ethiopia. In addition, the lifting of subsidies on basic goods and services, public expenditure cuts, tax reform and monetary contraction have contributed to urban poverty (Mekonen 1996; Tesfaye 2006)

The lack of adequate municipal services in many towns is widely noted. This is partly due to the weak institutional basis of municipalities. Municipalities in Ethiopia though established since the 1940s, lack sustained and comprehensive effort to strengthen their institutional capacity and improve their performance (Shewaye 2002) As a result, the major service delivery functions of municipalities did not receive enough attention in many municipalities. In order to address urban poverty, municipalities are expected to go even beyond the service delivery role and enhance local economic development by facilitating and coordinating the various actors: the private sector, civil society and the community. Until recently, urban areas do not have their autonomy within the decentralized system of local governments in Ethiopia. The recent move by some regions to grant autonomy and improve their capacity will help municipalities to fulfil their roles of urban poverty alleviation. Municipalities still need to be invigorated in order to address the livelihood problems of the urban poor. The urban poor for example do not consider municipalities as important institutions which is an indication of their limited role in the lives of the urban residents (Ellis and Tassew 2005).

Despite the ever deepening of urban poverty and numerous causes that fuel it, there is no sustained debate on urban poverty in Ethiopia (Abbi 2005). Some studies, however, have been undertaken addressing some dimensions of urban poverty. These studies could be divided into quantitative and qualitative (Abbi 2005). Among the quantitative studies, Mekonen (1996) estimated food poverty in urban Ethiopia on the basis of survey data from seven major urban centres and 1500 households. The study found the overall urban poverty line to be 15.09 birr per day or birr 72.88 per week per adult equivalent (which is 291.52 per month per household). According to the study, 39 per cent of the population in the urban centre is found to be below the poverty line. In a similar study, decomposition of poverty both by urban centre and household characteristics and the assessment of the dynamics and determinants of the poverty revealed that the poor are concentrated in the capital city, Addis Abeba, and in certain groups such as those with large household size and the uneducated (Mekonen 1999). Tesfaye (2006) analyzed total poverty line and found a very high incidence of poverty in urban Ethiopia. The study further decomposed changes in poverty indices into growth and redistribution effects. A decrease in mean consumption per adult during 1994 and 2000 led to a 3.1 percentage increase in head count index while redistribution favourable to the poor led to 1.4 percentage fall in poverty (Tesfaye 2006). The net effect was an increase of 1.7 per cent in head count index which is mostly a result of stronger adverse growth effect. Poverty levels are also found to be high among certain socio-economic groups.

The qualitative studies of urban poverty in Ethiopia are scant and few. Dessallegn and Aklilu (2002) used the livelihood security approach to study livelihood security as part of ILO study in four cities namely Addis Abeba, Adama, Mojo and Debre Zeit. The study found out that great majority of households experience livelihood insecurity, a threat of impoverishment and loss of means for basic sustenance. The study did not make its explicit goal to examine the relation between the livelihood requirements and poverty reduction programmes. A recent qualitative study is the participatory poverty assessment prepared for the Ministry of Finance and Economic Development intended to help the revision of the SDPRP (Ellis and Tassew 2005). This study examines both rural and urban poverty. In urban areas a total of 12 urban centres were selected for the study covering the regional capitals and other major urban centres. The main research themes were: livelihood trajectories, vulnerable groups, mobility and migration, institutional priorities and service delivery, empowerment and governance, gender dimension of poverty (ibid.). Under livelihood, the study found out that worse off people are those engaged in petty trading or are daily labourers and only a few people were upward moving (13 per cent) while a significant number of people (24 per cent) experienced a downward mobility. The reasons for downward mobility were illness, family size, decline in contraband trading, asset sales, divorce and increased competition. The youth, women and HIV infected were identified as vulnerable due to lack of skill, education and inability to start self employment. The most important institutions identified were the service giving institutions. Municipalities did not figure as important institutions. It was also found out that though people have now greater freedom of expression than in the past, social control is indicated to be high in urban Ethiopia.

The foregoing literature on urban poverty in Ethiopia provides insight into the complexities of the different dimensions of urban poverty. The quantitative studies are mostly preoccupied with estimating poverty line and they focus on income and consumption expenditure to understand well being. This, however, neglects the multidimensional nature of poverty. All the exercises are mostly done on big urban centres with very little information from small centres. Likewise, the qualitative studies also focus on big urban centres. Though the qualitative studies have thrown light on different aspects of livelihoods, there is little effort to present the different elements of livelihood such as shocks and coping strategies particularly at household level. In addition, there is no any effort to link livelihood requirements to the existing poverty reduction strategies at city level and how this could be improved in the future. This paper attempts to fill these gaps in the literature.

2.8 Summary of the Literature

Poverty has shown prominence in development discourse. There is now a consensus that pro-poor growth is needed to address the concerns of the poor. Increasingly, it has become clear that poverty is multidimensional. The income/consumption dimension of poverty, though critical, is not enough to understand poverty. Poverty has other dimensions involving human, socio-cultural, political and protective elements. A disaggregated measure of poverty is preferred because it reflects the reality and can be used in detailed planning and monitoring. The participatory poverty assessment has enabled to capture the perception of the poor and has given rise to the notions of vulnerability and powerlessness in understanding poverty.

The dimension of poverty along the rural/urban dimension is essential because the two show differences in incidence, economics, demography and politics. There is a tendency to underestimate urban poverty despite the fact that urban poverty has shown an increasing trend at national and international levels.

The livelihood framework, though originally, developed to study rural poverty can be used to understand urban poverty as well. The framework in particular helps to understand the strength of the poor in terms of asset possession and coping strategies. It also emphasizes the multidimensionality of poverty. The recognition that assets and strategies are influenced by institutions and policy helps to observe the macro-micro linkage.

The literature review has shown that urban poverty shows different characteristics along spectrum of towns. It also has shown that multiple-pronged strategies are needed to deal with the multidimensional poverty.

The Ethiopian literature on urban poverty underscores that there is limited debate on the issue by academic studies. The few studies available have focused on measuring poverty lines. They focus on big urban centres and do not detail household level. They also do not link livelihood requirements with existing urban poverty reduction policies and programme.

CHAPTER 3

THE SETTING: TOWNS AND HOUSEHOLDS

3.1 Towns Distribution and Characteristics

3.1.1 Distribution of Towns in Ethiopia

With 16 per cent of its total population (or 13 million people) living in urban areas, Ethiopia is under-urbanized compared to other African countries. The rates of urbanization which is on average 4 per cent, however, is very high and this will make the urban population in Ethiopia to exceed 50 million by 2050 (World Bank 2007).

Ethiopia has different cities with different status, mandates and sizes. The total number of cities and towns in the year 2006/07 was 925. In terms of status, there are two cities, namely Addis Ababa and Dire Dawa which are chartered cities and are directly accountable to the Federal Government. These cities have their own councils and are run as entities equivalent to regions. Each region contains cities designated as urban administrations that are accountable to regional governments and cities/towns that are directly under *woreda* administrations. The number of the urban administrations was 84 as of February 2007.

The size distribution of towns shows that out of 925 towns, 820 towns (or 89 per cent of the towns) have population size below 20,000. In our study regions, namely Amhara and Oromiya, there are 521 towns (89.4 per cent) with population size of less than 20,000 out of the total of 583 towns. The study regions are therefore equally dotted with numerous small towns as the national landscape. Towns over 200,000 are only one in each of the two study regions. These are Adama for Oromiya and Bhardar for the Amhara region. Other towns are in the size range of 20,000-200,000.

Table 3.1. Distribution of towns, by population size

Regional State / Federal Chartered City	Up to 2,000	2,000 to 4,999	5,000 to 19,999	20,000 to 49,999	50,000 to 99,000	100,000 to 200,000	Above 200,000	TOTAL
Amhara NRS	33	77	77	15	3	2	1	208
Oromia NRS	63	141	130	33	5	2	1	375
SNNP NRS	25	63	43	13	4	1		149
Tigray NRS	23	21	20	8	1	1		74
Afar NRS	12	9	6	1				28
Benshangul/Gumuz NRS	3	5	4	1				13
Gambella NRS	2	3	1	1				7
Somali NRS	10	20	28	7	1	1		67
Harari NRS						1		1
Addis Ababa City							1	1
Dire Dawa City			1				1	2
Totals	171	339	310	79	14	8	4	925
	18%	37%	34%	9%	2%	1%	0%	100%

SOURCE World Bank 2007

It is interesting to observe that the numerous small towns host fewer urban populations compared to the large towns. Table 3.2 shows that it is only 34 per cent of the urban population who live in towns of less than 20,000.

Tegegne Gebre-Egziabher

Table 3.2 Profile of urban population sizes, by regions (000)

Regional State / Federal Chartered City	Up to 4,999	5,000 to 19,999	20,000 to 49,999	50,000 to 99,000	100,000 to 200,000	Above 200,000	TOTAL
Addis Ababa charter City						3,059	3,059
Dire Dawa charter City		15				293	308
Oromia National Regional State	561	1,204	1,002	380	304	240	3,691
Amhara National Regional State	299	769	442	232	352	204	2,299
SNNP National Regional State	237	351	349	269	131		1,338
Tigray National Regional State	98	200	311	68	177		854
Somali National Regional State	77	277	239	71	105		767
Afar National Regional State	44	64	24				132
Harari National Regional State					127		127
Benshangul/Gumuz NRS	19	24	21				64
Gambella National Regional State	11	6	33				49
Totals	1,128	2,910	2,422	1,021	1,194	3,796	12,689
	11%	23%	19%	8%	9%	30%	100%

SOURCE: CSA (2006, January 2007). Projections from the 1994 Census.

The balance or 66 per cent live in towns of more than 20,000 people which account only for 11 per cent of the total number of towns. This is an indication that urban population in Ethiopia is concentrated in a few cities of the country.

3.1.2 Characteristics of Study Towns

3.1.2.1 Location and Administrative Status

Nine towns are included in this study. Eight of them are found in the two regions of Amhara and Oromiya (see Table 3.3 and Figure 1). The ninth city, Addis Ababa, is a federal capital and the capital city of the Oromiya region. All the small towns are found on the major road connecting Addis Ababa with the regional capitals-Assendabo is found on the Addis Ababa - Jimma road, Welenchiti is on the Addis-Dire Dawa road, Merawi is on Addis-Bahrdar road and Wuchale is on the Addis-Mekele road (see Fig. 2). All the small towns are also found between 30-60 kms from the nearest big city.

In terms of administrative status, the cities/towns are either *woreda* capitals, zonal capitals, or regional capitals. The administrative status helps towns to get access to services and infrastructure. The bigger cities, Bhardar, Dessie, Jimma and Adama, have attained city administration status while the small towns have municipal status (see Table 3.3 below for urban governance structure of the cities and towns).

Table 3.3 Some characteristics of study towns

Study town	Region	Administrative Status	Legal status	Size classification
Jimma	Oromiya	Zonal capital	City administration	Big town
Asendabo	Oromiya	*Woreda* capital	Municipal town	Small town
Adama	Oromiya	Zonal capital	City administration	Big town
Welenchiti	Oromiya	*Woreda* capital	Municipal town	Small town
Dessie	Amhara	Zonal capital	City administration	Big town
Wuchale	Amhara	*Woreda* capital	Municipal town	Small town
Bahirdar	Amhara	Regional capital	City administration	Big town
Merawi	Amhara	*Woreda* capital	Municipal town	Small town
Addis Ababa	Addis Ababa	National capital/ regional capital	Chartered city	Primate city

SOURCE: Own compilation

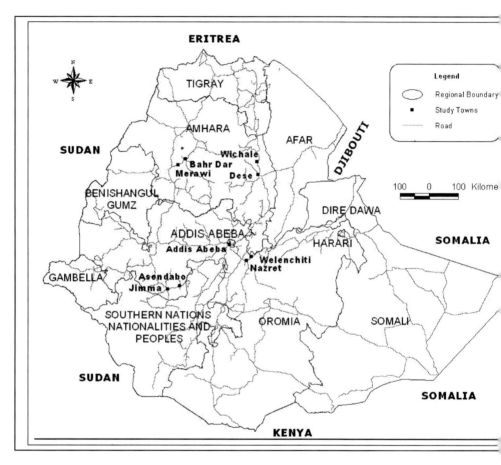

Figure 2. Map of the Study Towns

SOURCE: CSA. 1994.

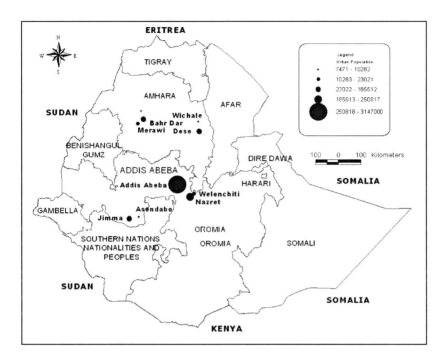

Figure 3. Map of the Study Towns, by Population Size

SOURCE: CSA. 1994

3.1.2.2 Demographic Profile

The nine towns vary by population size (see Fig. 3). According to various statistical reports, the four cities, namely Adama, Dessie, Bahirdar, and Jimma have had a population of over 100,000 in the last five years. Adama is the biggest, followed by Dessie, Bhardar and Jimma in that order. Out of the small towns, Welenchiti has a population of over 20,000 for most years. This could be due to the proximity of the town to Adama, which is the biggest commercial and service centre in the area. The other towns, particularly Wuchale and Asendabo, have population of about or less than 10,000 while Merawi stands in between these and Welenchiti (Table 3. 4).

Table 3.4 Population profile of study towns (2003-2007)

City/town	2003	2004	2005	2006	2007
Addis Ababa	2,805,000	2,887,000	2,973,000	3,059,000	3,147,000
Jimma	144,748	151,697	159,009	166,592	174,446
Adama	208,116	218,110	228,623	239,525	250,817
Bahrdar	152,787	159,793	167,261	175,185	183,489
Dessie	154,469	161,554	169,104	177,116	185,512
Assendabo	8,532	8,941	9,373	9,819	10,282
Welenchiti	19,102	20,019	20,984	21,985	23,021
Merawi	14,638	15,310	16,025	16,784	17,580
Wuchale	6,221	6,506	6,811	7,134	7,471

SOURCE, CSA Abstracts 2003-2007

Town growth is caused by numerous factors namely demographic growth, migration and re-classification. According to the 2005 labour force survey, the contribution of migration to urban population growth is found to be significant. Migrants form nearly 50 per cent of the urban population at national level (Table 3.5). The picture is similar for the regions where the study towns are found. In fact, in the Amhara region, the proportion of migrants (54.50 per cent) is slightly higher than that of the national average.

Table 3.5 Summary of population size vs. migrants, by number and
            percentage

	Urban population	No. of migrants	Per cent of migrants
Country	8,974,598	4,436,478	49.43
Addis Ababa	2,116,202	919,379	43.44
Amhara region	1,607,996	876,513	54.50
Oromiya region	2,715,475	1,338,864	49.30

SOURCE: Labour Force Survey, 2005

In all study towns, females generally form nearly half of the total urban population (Table 3.6). Addis Ababa, Wuchale and Merawi have female population that is slightly in excess of the male population.

Table 3.6 Gender composition of study towns' population, 2006-2007

	2006			2007		
	Total urban population	No. of females	Per cent of females	Total	No. of females	Per cent of females
A.A	3,059,000	1,590,000	51.97	3,147,000	1,636,000	51.98
Jimma	166592	81829	49.11	174446	85680	49.11
Adama	239525	119811	50.00	250817	125449	50.01
Bahrdar	175185	84737	48.37	183489	88790	48.38
Dessie	177116	86865	49.04	185512	91019	49.06
Assendabo	9819	4916	50.06	10282	5147	50.05
Welenchıtı	21985	10936	49.74	23021	11450	49.73
Merawi	16784	8857	52.77	17580	9281	52.79
Wuchale	7134	3650	51.16	7471	3824	51.18

SOURCE: CSA Abstracts (2006, 2007)

3.1.2.3 Social and Municipal Services

Social services include education and health services. Most of the small towns have elementary and junior schools. They also have either senior secondary school or preparatory school though their number is limited to one in each town. Health services are mostly limited to health posts or health stations. Municipal services in small towns are very rudimentary or unavailable. For example, none of the towns has solid waste disposal system and only one town has abattoir service and another one town has a bus-station. Water service is inadequate though in some towns such as Asendabo the severity is extreme. The standards of internal road in all small towns are inadequate.

Big towns are better provided with social and municipal services. This could be due to the fact that higher population concentration requires a higher level of service. Alternatively, municipalities of big towns have higher levels of resources which enable them to provide a better service compared to small towns. Solid waste disposal and sewerage, however, are insufficient in most towns.

3.1.2.4 Poverty and Unemployment

Table 2.4 in chapter 2 provided the poverty incidence of the five big towns of the study. In 2004/05, the levels of poverty ranged from 30 per cent in Adama and Bahrdar to 33 per cent in A.A and Dessie. Jimma occupies an intermediate level of 32 per cent these levels of poverty, though slightly lower than the national urban poverty level of 35 per cent, are still high.

What is more worrying, however, is that most of these towns (Jimma, Adama and Addis Ababa) have exhibited an increase in their levels of poverty over the period 1995/96-2004/05. As can be seen in **Table 3.7,** unemployment rate in the five towns range from 19 per cent in Bahirdar to 31 per cent in Addis Ababa. The national urban unemployment rate, according to the 2005 labour force survey, was 20.6 per cent.

Table 3.7 Unemployment rates of big towns

	Male	Female	Total
Dessie	17.8	36.6	27.4
Bahirdar	9.8	25.7	18.7
Adama	17.5	30.7	24.6
Jimma	12.9	30.2	21.5
Addis Ababa	24.3	37.7	31.3

SOURCE: Labour force survey, 2005

3.2 Households' Structure and Access to Basic Services

Households come in different shapes and sizes. They vary in different characteristics, such as demographic features, ethnicity, occupation, etc. Understanding the demographic profile of urban poverty is critical to target policy interventions effectively (Muzzine 2008). This is because different demographic features provide different opportunities and constraints for livelihood strategies of the poor and their capacity to lift themselves out of poverty (*ibid.*). Household structure and composition in the form of household size, dependency ratio and sex of household head have implications for poverty reductions and needs of the family.

3.2.1 Demographic Features of Households

Among the demographic features, the sex, age and marital status of household heads are presented in Table 3.8. The majority (53.6 per cent) of the households are female-headed households. This corresponds with the results of PASDEP (MoFED 2006) which reported that in urban Ethiopia female-headed households are much higher than in rural areas with the order of magnitude being 41per cent against 23 per cent. Female-headed households have higher incidence, depth and severity of poverty compared to their counterparts (*ibid.*). This is due to limited opportunities females face in comparison to males. In terms of age distribution, most of the household heads (55.4 per cent) lie within the age range of 31-55 years of age. This is the most productive age in the life cycle of individuals. A significant proportion (31 per cent) however, is found in the old age group of above 55 years of age. Married couples are pre dominant (51.0 per cent) in the study sample. Among household members, there are fewer infants

(7.7 per cent) and children (23.9 per cent). The number of adults with age range between 15 and 59 is quite high. This accounts for the low dependency ratio in the study population. The dependency ratio for the sample population is found to be 0.52, which is lesser than the dependency ration found in other studies in urban areas. For example, Muzzine (2008) found a dependency ratio of 1.0 in urban areas.

Table 3.8 Characteristics of household heads, by age, sex and marital status

	Frequency	Per cent
Sex		
Male	230	46.4
Female	266	53.6
	496	100
Age		
20-30	68	13.7
31-40	116	23.4
41-55	158	32.0
>55	154	30.9
Total	496	100
Marital status		
Married	253	51.0
Single	152	30.6
Divorced	35	7.1
Separated	56	11.3
Total	496	100

SOURCE: Own Survey

3.2.2 Household Migration Status

Among the sample households, only 36 per cent were born in the town (Table 3.9). A little less than two-third (64 per cent) are therefore migrants or were not born in the town, or had moved over from other places. The fact that the majority of the sample households are migrants is an indication that urbanization in Ethiopia is fuelled by migration.

Table 3.9 Migration status, by sex and level of education

	Migrant	Non-migrant
Sex		
Male	42.9	44.6
	(136)*	(82)
Female	57.1	55.4
	(181)	(102)
Total	100	100
	(317)	(184)
Level of education		
None	45.7	37.0
Read and write only	19.6	12.0
Primary	13.2	12.0
Junior secondary	7.9	15.8
Secondary	9.8	19.6
Diploma	2.8	1.6
Degree	0.3	1.1
Other	0.6	1.1
Total	100	100

SOURCE: Own survey

*Figures in parenthesis are numbers

The majority of migrants are females though this is also true for the non-migrants as well. A significant proportion of the migrants (33 per cent) can read and write or have attained a primary level education. Non-migrants in this category are 24 per cent. It is interesting to note, however, that a significant proportion of non-migrants (35.4 per cent) have attained a junior or senior secondary level of education while migrants in this category are only 18 per cent. The possible reason for this could be that migrants may not have a luxury of going to higher level education as they have to fetch for themselves as opposed to non-migrants who could be easily supported by families or relatives most likely living in the town or city.

A very significant proportion of the migrants (69 per cent) have come from rural areas while it is only 30 per cent who migrated from other urban areas. Rural-urban migration is therefore the dominant mode of migration. Most of the migrants are long-term migrants. They have a long duration of stay. About 85 per cent of the migrants have stayed in their current town of residence for more than 8 years. The longer the duration of stay of migrants, the lesser their relation with their rural origin.

Job-related and family-related reasons stood out as the two most important reasons for migration as, together, they accounted for 86 per cent of the responses. Job-related reasons or mainly searching for jobs accounted for 55 per cent of the responses. For rural people, migration is the best or the only option to find work. Rural people move to both small and big cities in search of jobs. While rural people move to cities and towns in search of jobs, in reality, however, what they often find could be contrary to their expectation. Since most towns and cities do not have the capacity to absorb them, they find themselves in a state of poverty. Family-related reasons were found to be important in this study. This involves people's movement for marriage reasons, following relatives or due to family problems.

With regard to migration status by group of towns, it was found that the proportion of migrants in big towns (70 per cent) is higher than those in Addis Ababa (60 per cent) and in small towns (58 per cent) (see Table 3.10). The big towns are mostly regional capitals (e.g, Bahirdar) or important secondary cities in their respective regions (Adama, Dessie, Jimma). They thus receive a high number of migrants. Though Addis Ababa is a major attraction point for migrants from all over the country, the proximity of big and secondary towns for those with rural origin could be one reason for their dominance. Differences with respect to number of migrants among towns are significant at 95 per cent   level of confidence (A chi-square value of 6.94 at 2 degrees of freedom).

As far as causes for migration are concerned, job-related reason were found to be more important in big towns (56 per cent) and in Addis Ababa (64 per cent) as opposed to small towns (50 per cent) In contrast, family-related reasons are more dominant factors in small towns (37 per cent) compared to big towns (25 per cent) and Addis Ababa (33 per cent). In some small towns like Asendabo (50 per cent) and Welenchit (45.7 per cent), family-related reasons were the major causes for a significant majority of migrants. These reasons show statistically significant difference among the groups of towns (chi-square value = 24.08, df=12). The fact that family-related reasons are more important in small towns is an indication that migration to smaller town is driven by social forces rather than economic forces. Small towns have less capacity to provide employment opportunity. Other reasons, such as education, health and security, were found to be of less importance in all towns.

Table 3.8 Migration status, by group of towns (%)

	Small towns	Big towns	A.A	Total	Chi square
Proportion of migrants	58	70	60	63.3	Value= 6.94 df =2
Reasons for migration					
Family reason	36.9	25.0	33.0	30.9	Value= 24.08 df= 12
Security related	3.6	2.1	1.7	2.6	
Housing related	3.6	2.9	0.0	2.6	
In search of job	49.5	55.7	63.3	55.0	
Health reason	2.7	0.7	0.0	1.3	
Education reason	2.7	4.3	1.7	3.2	
Other	0.1	9.3	0.0	4.5	
Total	100	100	100	100	

SOURCE: Own survey

3.2.3 Access to Economic and Social Infrastructure

Economic and social infrastructure provision is closely related to human capital development (Moser 1998). Education service ensures that people gain skill and knowledge while economic infrastructure, such as water, transport and electricity, helps people to use their skills and knowledge productively.

Proximity, provision and accessibility are among aspects of service delivery. In general, towns and cities provide some level of services within their boundary. Thus, as shown above, education, health, and electric power supply are some of the basic infrastructures found in the study towns and cities. In this sub-section we examine access to economic and social infrastructure by the poor.

3.2.3.1 Access to Education and Health

Access to both education and health are generally not easy for the poor. In the case of education, a significant proportion (30.2 per cent) indicated that access to primary education was difficult, or very difficult (25 per cent). Similarly, 33.9 per cent and 48.5 per cent mentioned that enrolling their children in secondary school was 'difficult' and 'very difficult', respectively (see Figure 4). It is quite true that education is provided freely in public schools. However, there are many accompanying costs that make access difficult and beyond the reach of the poor households. These include expenses for of school uniform and educational materials, such as text books, exercise books, stationeries, etc. which are borne by households. These costs become particularly prohibitive for households with large family size. In addition to the costs of education, distance to schools could also make access difficult.

Concerning health, access to government health services was found to be better than access to private health facilities. In total, 36.3 per cent mentioned that access to government health facility was either 'very easy' or 'easy' (see Figure 5). Those who responded the same for private health facilities were only 7.8 per cent. This is an indication that access to private health facilities is beyond the reach of the poor. In fact, 72 per cent responded by saying that gaining access to a private facility was 'very difficult' while those who mentioned access to government facility as 'very difficult' were only 17 per cent (see Figure 5).

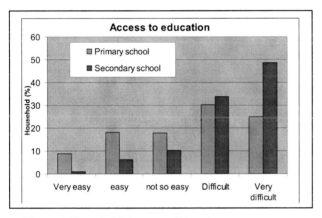

Figure 4. Household Access to Education

SOURCE: Own survey

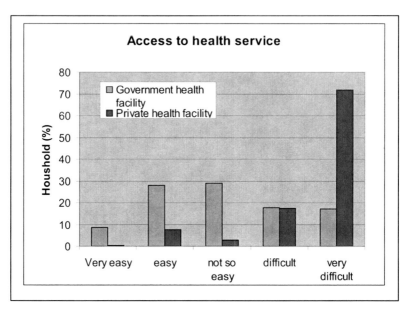

Figure 5. Households Access to Health Service

SOURCE: Own survey

3.2.3.2 Access to Safe Drinking Water

In general, about 89 per cent of the households indicated that they have access to clean water, and only 11 per cent mentioned having no access to clean water. It was found that households in small towns have relatively lower level of access than those in bigger towns. In other words, only 74 per cent reported having access to safe water in small towns as opposed to 98 per cent in bigger towns, and 99 per cent in Addis Ababa. In some small towns, the number of those with no access to safe drinking water is even very high. For instance, in Asendabo almost all (98 per cent) respondents indicated that they have difficulties in getting clean water for drinking purposes.

In Ethiopia, as shown in Table 3.11, urban towns are provided with safe drinking water better than rural areas. According to the Ministry of Water Resources, access to safe drinking water in urban areas is defined if people can get access to water within 500 meters (MoWR 2008). In urban places access to safe drinking water is, on average, 86 per cent. The fact that the big towns in this study have a higher proportion of households with access to drinking water indicates that these towns are better served than others. It is surprising, however, to see that nearly all the sample households in Asendabo mentioned that they have no access to drinking water while the regional average for urban Oromiya, to which Asendabo belongs, is 98 per cent.

Table 3.9 Summary profile of access to safe drinking water in 2007/8

No	Regions	Rural	Urban	Total
1	Tigray	56	72	59.1
2	Afar	53.1	77.4	55.4
3	Amhara	49	87.8	53.7
4	Oromiya	52	97.9	58.3
5	Somali	32.9	61.6	37.9
6	Benishngul Gumuz	44.3	93.1	49.3
7	SNNPR	63	72.1	63.6
8	Gambella	43.9	98.6	54.7
9	Harari	27.5	41	32.5
10	Diredawa	75.8	72	73
11	Addis Ababa		95	95
12	National	53.9	86.2	59.5

SOURCE: Ministry of Water Resources (2008)

3.2.3.3 Access to Safe Waste Disposal

The study revealed that access to safe disposal of waste is not easy for the majority of the study population. About 52 per cent mentioned having no access to disposal of waste. However, there is great variation among cities and towns. In small towns the proportion of households with access to safe disposal of waste is only 27 per cent as opposed to 55 per cent in Addis Ababa, and 59 per cent in big towns. The variation within small towns is also high. For instance, Merawi (16.3 per cent) and Welenchiti (10 per cent) have very small proportion of their households with access to safe disposal, compared to Asendabo and Wuchale, each with 40 per cent of the households having access. Among the big towns, Jimma and Dessie also have a small proportion of their households with access to waste disposal. The fact that access to disposal of waste is limited in urban areas indicates that environmental hazards characterize urban life as opposed to rural life (Moser 1998). Environmental hazards have a particularly serious impact upon the urban poor human capital, health and well being (*ibid.*).

3.2.3.4 Sources of Cooking and Lighting

The main source of lighting for households in this study is electricity. Nearly half (49 per cent) of the households use shared electric power while 44 per cent use private power supplies (meters), as shown in Figure 6 below. Firewood and charcoal are the main sources of energy for cooking. A substantial proportion (54 per cent) of the households use both firewood and charcoal for cooking, while another 22 per cent use firewood only

(Figure 7). This has substantial environmental implication that merits a closer study on the relation between urban poverty and the environment.

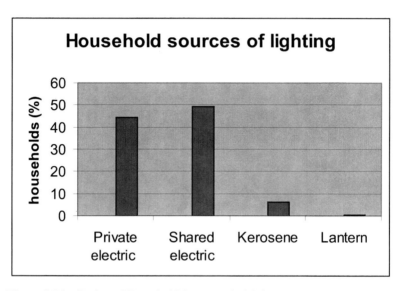

Figure 6. Distribution of Household Sources of Lighting

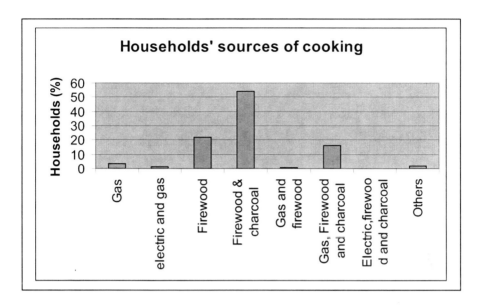

Figure 7. Distribution of Households' Sources of Cooking

SOURCE: Own survey

Summary

Ethiopia has low levels of urbanization but has fast rates of urban growth. Rural-urban migration is a significant component of urbanization in Ethiopia. It is understandable from city size distribution that most (89 per cent) cities in Ethiopia are small towns with population sizes of less than 20,000. These cities house only one-third of the total urban population. The balance is found in big cities which are fewer in number. The small towns have limited municipal and social services. Poverty data particularly for the big cities of the study show that these cities are among those with the highest incidence of poverty and unemployment.

Background data on study households reveal that female-headed households are in the majority; most household heads are in their productive age, and married couples are predominant. A little less than two-thirds are migrants mainly from rural areas. This highlights the importance of rural-urban migration in Ethiopian urbanization. City difference is observed both in the levels of and reasons for migration. The big towns in this study, which are either regional capitals or secondary cities, have a higher proportion of migrants than Addis Ababa or small towns. This shows the attractive power of regional centres which are found in the middle of rural areas. In terms of reasons, job related reasons are dominant in Addis Ababa and big towns as opposed to small towns in which family related reasons seem to dominate.

Access to social and economic infrastructure has implication for human capital development. In this regard, the study found that, in general, access to education and health is not easy, though access to government education and health facilities is better. Access to drinking water was also found to be very difficult in small towns, while access to safe disposal was difficult in all the towns. Households predominantly use firewood and charcoal for cooking and this highlights the need to study the relation between urban poverty and the environment.

CHAPTER 4
URBAN LIVELIHOODS

4.1 Asset Status of Urban Households

Assets are the core of the household strategies to survive, meet their future needs or reduce their exposure to risks. Their asset portfolios determine their level of resilience and responsiveness to risks, shocks and events. Asset portfolios are linked to livelihood strategies through households' management of their assets. A certain type of assets could be used to secure other assets as in the case of education being used to secure income (financial asset) or financial assets being used to secure education and skill. Similarly, social assets may entitle households access to credit, food or other aspects of livelihood. Households may also deplete their assets to secure their livelihood because of no other better options. This is not a sustainable strategy and leads the poor to a vicious circle of poverty. In general, assets are not only inputs to livelihood but also outputs (Bebbington 1999). Assets are transformable and the transformation depends on households' decision influenced by internal power relations, exposure to stress and emergencies, the social identity of its members and the stage of the domestic life cycle (Schutte 2004). The livelihood approach requires an understanding of the assets in order to identify the opportunities they may provide and the constraints they pose (Rakodi 2002a).

4.1.1 Physical Assets

Physical assets are understood here to mean both productive and household assets. The former includes, among others, tools and equipments households may use to generate income, livestock they possess and houses they own. Household assets refer to the various durable and non-durable items but in particular to valuables. Valuables such as jewelleries and other saleable are hedges or insurance against risk.

4.1.1.1 Productive assets

Equipment and Tools

Equipment and tools are important assets to generate income. Tools, such as handicraft tools and looms, enhance labour productivity and enable households to manufacture products for sale or consumption. In this study, it was revealed that that the poor do not own much equipment and tools that could be used to generate income or enhance labour productivity. Tools like sewing machine, handicraft loom and others were reported by a very insignificant number of households (see Table 4.1). Hence there was no difference among towns in this regard. The lack of equipment and tools is an indication that household income is not supported by these sources. It also indicates that since the use of these tools requires skill, their absence may indicate the lack of such skills.

Livestock

It is understandable that livestock and livestock products can be significant sources of income in urban areas. Livestock products such as dairy products are in great demand in urban areas and they could generate lucrative income for the poor to support their livelihood. In our study, however, it was revealed that this is not available for the majority of the poor. Livestock possession was reported only by 10 per cent of the total households. However, households in some towns seem to have a higher possession of livestock than others. For example, in Welenchiti and Asendabo towns, 34 per cent and 22 per cent of the households respectively have livestock as opposed to towns such as Addis Ababa, Dessie, Bahir Dar where no ownership of livestock was reported (Table 4.1).

In general, households in small towns seem to have a better possession of livestock resource than those in big cities. On average, nearly 20 per cent of the households in small towns own livestock resources as opposed to 6.2 per cent in big towns and none in Addis Ababa. The close proximity of small towns to rural areas could be one of the reasons for a higher number of households possessing livestock. Livestock asset can thus be used as a source of income in the small towns. On the other hand, absence of livestock in big towns is surprising since the demand for livestock products is expected to be higher in big towns than in small towns.

Housing as an Asset

Housing is the most valuable single possession of the poor in urban areas. In urban areas, housing is equated with land for rural people. House is an asset that can be used not only to protect oneself from the vagaries of weather but is also an important asset on which income generating activities can be based. For example, home-based enterprises are important for home-bound households (Moser 1998). Renting house is also an important source of income (*ibid.*).

In the focus group discussion, house was identified as one of the assets of the poor. The others being health, children, and own labour. The house mentioned could be own house in some cases, or *kebele* owned house in other cases.

In the household data it was found that possession of house was reported by high proportion (22 per cent). There is, however, variation across cities. Asendabo, Welenchiti and Jimma are towns with nearly 40 per cent or more of households reporting house possession. In all other towns, house possession was below 40 per cent, while in Bahir Dar none reported house possession.

In general, there is a higher level of house possession in small towns (34.7 per cent) than in big towns (16.3 per cent) and Addis Ababa (7.1 per cent). In small towns, easy access to land could be one reason that encourages people to own houses. For instance in Wuchale it was reported that there was no one on the waiting list for land as all those who can afford to construct houses are provided with land (personal communication). On the other hand, even if land is available in big cities, its affordability excludes the poor from having land. In Addis Ababa, for example one has to deposit a sum of nearly 15,000 birr (US$ 1765) for 175m^2 of land and 8,000 birr (US $ 941) for 94m^2 of land. Low income households cannot afford to pay such amount. It is only 20 per cent of the households in Addis Ababa who can afford to put up such payments (Assefa and Tegegne 2008).

In some towns even if house ownership was reported, it is not clear whether those who reported have land titles. In many cities in Ethiopia, people occupy land but do not have land title. Under such circumstances, tenure security is under question and vulnerability to policy changes is high.

Most of those who own houses (67.5 per cent) built the houses with own money while 17.5 per cent have inherited the house. The fact that most use own money is an indication of the poor housing finance in Ethiopia. Since people's capacity is limited, the use of own money will usually result in the construction of low quality housing.

Table 4.1. Possession of productive asset by households in different towns (percentage)

	Small towns	Big towns	Addis Ababa	Total
House	34.7	16.3	7.1	21.8
Livestock	19.4	6.2	0.0	10.0
Car	2.2	0.5	1.0	1.3
Sewing machine	4.8	1.5	1.0	2.7
Handicraft loom	1.6	0.0	1.0	0.8

SOURCE: Own survey

Since housing is an important asset for urban households, it is essential to understand its different dimensions. First, it is vital to see the tenure type because of its direct implications for poverty. Second, the quality of housing which is a direct indicator of the standard of living and the possibility for using housing for income generating activities needs to be understood.

In terms of tenure, there are different tenure types or modes of house occupation. Rent and ownership are the two most dominant modes of occupation. People can also live for free in government, relative or other organization's house or live in charity houses. Within rental tenure, there are different kinds of landlords. The most common ones are private and public (Rakodi 1995). In the Ethiopian case, the landlords could be *kebeles*, municipalities, housing agencies or private individuals. Except for the latter, all the landlords are public.

In the study area, there are two dominant tenure types. Owner occupied[4] (24 per cent) and rental occupation (73.2 per cent) (see Table 4.2). Those living in rent free houses are insignificant (2.6 per cent). The proportion of households who live in their own houses is lower than what was reported in the 2004 national Welfare Monitoring Survey (WMS). The WMS reported that 43 per cent of households in urban areas live in their own house. The difference is understandable since our study was conducted in poor neighbourhood and those in the sample were poor households. The proportion of households renting houses is higher in big towns (76.3 per cent) and Addis Ababa (92 per cent) than in small towns (60.8 per cent). On the contrary, those living in own houses are higher (38 per cent) in small towns than in big towns (19 per cent) and Addis Ababa (6 per cent). The difference in tenure type among towns is statistically significant (Chi-square value = 57.12; df=10).

This result falls in line with other studies which have investigated the relation between tenure type and city size. For instance, in Indonesia it was found that 30 per cent of households in Jakarta were tenants compared to 22 per cent in all large cities, 31 per cent in medium cities, and 16 per cent in small cities (Hoffman et al. 1991). Similarly, in India the proportion of households who were tenants was higher in the cities with a population of 1 million or more (61 per cent) than settlements between 5,000 and 10,000 inhabitants (32 per cent) (Wadhva 1990). It therefore seems that rental tenure is significant in big towns compared to small towns. There are several factors that go towards explaining the importance of rental tenure in big towns. The supply of land for housing, oligopolistic ownership and high prices in relation to income and capital available constrain housing production, and force a higher proportion of urban households in big towns to rent (Rakodi 1995). Rental tenure entails insecurity and will make it difficult for the poor to use housing as a productive unit.

Table 4.2 Tenure type of households, by group of towns (percentage)

	Small towns	Big towns	Addis Ababa	Total
Owner occupied	37.7	18.8	6.1	23.8
Rented from kebele	49.2	61.9	86.9	61.8
Rented from municipality	0.5	1.0	0.0	0.6
Rented from private households	11.1	13.4	5.1	10.8
Rent free	1.0	4.5	2.0	2.6
Others	0.5	0.5	0.0	0.4
N	199	200	99	498
			Chi square value = 57.12; df =10	

SOURCE: Own survey

Among those households who rent houses, most (62 per cent) live in houses rented from *kebele* (Table 4.2). The proportion of those households living in *kebele* houses in A.A is much higher (87 per cent) than those in big towns (62 per cent), and those in small towns (49 per cent). *Kebele* houses are subsidized houses. These are houses which were confiscated by the government during the military rule in Ethiopia and were put under the responsibility of *kebeles*. The houses are usually poorly constructed and poorly maintained. Nearly 84 per cent of the houses were built more than 20 years ago. Houses with such long period of service require frequent maintenance.

The *kebele* houses are rented for a very small amount of money. For instance, in this study it was found that the average amount of rent paid was 15 birr per month. There are, however, people who pay as low as 1 birr or 0.50 cents per month. Those who rent from private individuals pay market rent and this is much higher than the *kebele* rental amount. Their number however is small (11 per cent). Rental tenure poses a demand to generate income and in some instances it may even lead to the accumulation of debt among the poor.

Quality of housing is a reflection of different attributes of houses. These pertain to size or floor area, number of rooms, construction materials and whether houses have shared structures or not, etc.

The findings in this study revealed that the majority (59 per cent) of the poor in all the study areas live in non-storied, attached houses (see Figure 8). These kinds of houses are relatively cheaper to construct because of common walls between houses. Non-storied detached houses are the second most prevalent types of houses (39 per cent). Other types of houses, particularly multi-story houses, are insignificant.

The overwhelming majority (94 per cent) of households in Addis Ababa live in non-storied attached houses while it is nearly half of the households who live in the same type of houses in small towns (49 per cent) and big towns (52 per cent). The other half (49 per cent) of households in small towns and big towns (47 per cent) live in non-storied detached houses. The difference between towns is statistically significant at the highest level of confidence (Chi-square value= 72.34, df=8). The fact that most households in Addis Ababa live in non-storied attached houses indicates the severity of housing shortages in Addis Ababa. For example, according to the Addis Ababa City Master Plan, the housing backlog in 2002 was 233,000 (Addis Ababa City Government 2002). It is estimated that by 2010, 223, 000 additional units will be needed (*ibid.*). This is not the case in small towns, such as Merawi, where the majority (85 per cent) live in detached houses.

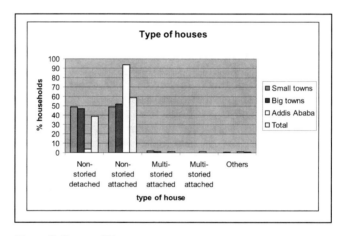

Figure 8. Types of Houses

As shown in Table 4.3, the mean floor area of all houses ranges between $14m^2$-$36m^2$ with the average for all towns being $24m^2$. Such floor area is very small in light of the size of the households. It was earlier indicated that the average family size in the study areas is 4.3 but the average family size reaches 6 in Jimma and 5.5 in Addis Ababa.

Most (86.5 per cent) of the houses in the study areas have one or two rooms and about 40 per cent of the households live in one room. The average number of rooms is 1.8. This is slightly less than what is reported in the Welfare Monitoring Survey report of 2004. The report indicates that the average number of rooms to be 2.21 in urban areas. The number of rooms has to be seen in light of the number of occupants. It is an indicator of the state of crowdedness. Given the household size in this study, we can conclude that houses are over-crowded in the study area. Another study has also concluded that, with close to two-thirds of dwelling units having one or two rooms, houses in Addis Ababa are over-crowded (Assefa and Tegegne 2008).

Also, as indicated in Table 4.3, housing condition in terms of floor size and number of rooms seems to be better in small towns than in bigger towns or Addis Ababa. There is, however, a general similarity in the types of construction materials. About 98 per cent of the houses have walls made of mud and wood, 97.2 per cent have corrugated iron as a roof, 79 per cent have earthen floor and wall, and 59 per cent have no ceiling. There is a striking similarity among different cities and towns regarding the quality of housing. The poor who live in such poor quality housing cannot use houses as basis for income generating activities.

Table 4.3 Profile of housing condition, by towns

	Small towns	Big towns	A.A	Total
Average floor size (m2)	27.36	21.16	21.80	23.8
Average number of rooms	2.04	1.73	1.51	1.81
Walls made of mud and wood	97.5	98.0	99.0	98.0
Corrugated iron roof	96.4	97.5	98.0	97.2
Mud floor	88.8	80.1	58.0	79.1

SOURCE: Own survey

Facilities and Amenities in the House

The three most important sources of drinking water for households, in their order of importance, are: public taps (or 'bono' water, as they are locally known) (41.1 per cent), private vendors (21.1per cent), and private meter (19.6 per cent) (see Table 4.4). The importance of these three sources of water varies by city size. The differences are statistically significant (Chi-square =188.7; df= 12).

'Bono' water is predominant in Merawi, Asendabo and Wuchale, which are all small towns. In fact, 62 per cent of the households in small towns source water from public taps. Purchasing water from private vendors is more dominant in Jimma, Adama and Bhardar, with 37 per cent of households in big towns deriving water from this source. Households with private meter seem to be more in Addis Ababa (37.4 per cent). Slightly over one-third of the households in Addis Ababa and Welenchiti get water from private meter. In all other towns the proportion of households obtaining water from this source is much lower. One of the reasons is the lack of affordability, as water connection requires upfront payment which is beyond the reach of the poor.

In general, public fountains seem to be the dominant source of water for households in small towns. In big towns buying from vendors, public taps and shared meter outside the compound are important. In Addis Ababa, private meter and buying from vendors are main sources. It thus appears that those households in big towns and Addis Ababa have more diversified sources of water. In terms of improved water, some studies consider shared source and public fountains as unimproved water (Muzzuni 2008). If this is the case, then, it is only a very small proportion (16 per cent) of households in small town who have access to improved water.

Table 4.4. Distribution of water sources of households, by percentage

	Small towns	Big towns	A.A	Total
Private meter	16.4	14.0	37.0	19.6
Shared within compound	6.2	0.5	3.0	3.2
Shared outside compound	4.6	24.5	1.0	11.9
Public taps ('Bono water')	62.1	24.0	34.3	41.1
Buying from private vendor	3.1	37.0	24.2	21.1
Protected well or sprig	0.5	0.0	0.0	0.2
Unprotected well or spring	7.2	0.0	0.0	2.8
N	195	200	99	494
	Chi-square value 188.7, df = 12			

SOURCE: Own survey

In terms of toilets, a significant proportion (24 per cent) of the households reported that they had no toilet facility). This implies that night soil flows freely, posing great health risks. Those with no toilet facilities are very high in Merawi (66 per cent), and Assendabo (53 per cent), which are both small towns. In general 38 per cent of households in small towns, 16 per cent in big towns and 10 per cent in Addis Ababa have no toilet facilities. Among those who have toilet facility, shared dry pit latrine is the major (31.5 per cent) form of toilet facility. The highest in this regard being in big towns (46 per cent) and Addis Ababa (35 per cent). In addition to the above problem of toilet, 96 per cent of all respondents reported that they have no bathing facility. Bathing is therefore taken in other places outside the house or in inappropriate places. A significant proportion (37.5 per cent) has no separate kitchen as well. The problem is more sever in small towns (47 per cent), followed by big towns (39 per cent) than in Addis Ababa (17 per cent). These households must be using their houses or open air for cooking purposes. Nearly 62 per cent of the households have traditional kitchens, while some (24.2 per cent) households share these traditional kitchens.

Solid waste disposal facilities are practically absent in small towns, with the majority (58.2 per cent) throwing away their wastes (Table 4.5). A significant proportion (35 per cent) use dug-outs to dispose of their wastes. Bigger towns and Addis Ababa fare better in waste collection since 65 per cent and 53 per cent respectively use communal collection bins (Table 4.5). A new trend in Addis Ababa is the use of waste collecting micro enterprises serving nearly 17 per cent of the households. These enterprises collect waste from houses and take them to collection centres. This act supports the municipality and creates employment for those engaged in the enterprises. The fact that there is a highly significant statistically difference in waste collection facilities points to the need to focus attention on this issue particularly in small towns.

Table 4.5 Solid waste disposal facilities in towns (%)

	Small towns	Big towns	A.A	Total
Communal collection ('Genda')	4.1	64.6	52.5	38.1
Dug out	34.7	3.0	0.0	15.0
Throwing away	58.2	21.2	29.3	37.5
Collected by MSEs	0.0	0.0	17.2	3.4
Others	3.1	11.1	1.0	5.9
N	196	198	99	493
Chi square value -307.4, df-8				

SOURCE: Own survey

4.1.1.2 Household Assets

Possession of household asset indicates not only the standard of living enjoyed by the poor but also the possibilities of using them as insurance or hedge against shocks. In all towns, video and audio electric appliances are owned by a higher proportion of households than other types of assets such as refrigerators, jewellery, etc (Table 4.6). A higher proportion of households in Addis Ababa reported possession of these household assets than households in other towns. It can then be said that for more than one-fifth of the households these assets can be used as securities in times of need. These items, however, are not highly durable and can easily lose value. Jewellery, however, which is an important store of wealth and which is highly liquid, is an exception rather than the norm among the households. It is only 5.8 per cent who own some kind of jewellery and this goes down to as low as 2.0 per cent in Addis Ababa (Table 4.6). In general it does not appear that households have significant assets to fall back on in times of emergency or shocks.

Table 4.6 Distribution of possession of household assets (%)

Type of Physical Assets	Small towns	Big towns	A.A	Total
TV	28.7	27.6	73.0	37.4
Radio	21.1	31.6	16.0	24.3
Tape recorder	37.9	31.1	60.6	39.8
Telephone	20.6	15.2	41.0	22.6
Refrigerator	4.9	3.6	13.0	6.0
Jewellery	8.6	5.1	2.0	5.8
Sofa	6.5	5.1	28.0	10.4
Electric baking pan ("mitad")[5]	1.1	2.1	23.0	6.1

SOURCE: Own survey

4.1.2 Financial Assets

Financial assets refer to the financial resource base of the poor. It includes income, transfers, savings, as well as credit. Income is the most important financial asset. Income data, however, are very difficult to obtain as people are not willing to disclose their earnings. The following looks at savings and credit situation of households.

4.1.2.1 Savings

The study found that only 14 per cent of the urban poor save from their income (Table 4.7). In small towns, 14.4 per cent reported savings while in big towns and Addis Ababa those who reported savings were 13.6 per cent and 13.0 per cent respectively. The proportions of households with savings are not statistically different between towns (see chi-square value in table 4.7). Two observations can be made from the figures. First, saving rate is very low, indicating that the majority of the poor have no saving capacity which, in turn, is partly a reflection of the meagre amount of income of the poor. Second, saving rate among the poor is similar irrespective of where the poor live.

The amount of savings, however, is statistically different among the towns. While the average amount of saving is 1302 birr, households in small towns reported a higher amount of savings (2107.74 birr) (Table 4.7). The average amount of saving in big towns is 718.8 birr and the average in Addis Ababa (214 birr) is even much lower than that of the big towns. Since saving is a function of income, the poor in small towns should be better off than those either in big towns or Addis Ababa.

Table 4.7 Distribution of households savings and place of savings (%)

	Small towns	Big towns	Addis Ababa	Total	
Proportion of Households with savings	14.4	13.6	13.0	13.8	Chi-square Value =0.123; df =2
Place of savings					
'Equib' (rotating saving)	42.39	43.8	7.1	37.0	Chi-square value = 16.62; df= 8
Bank	17.1	12.5	7.1	13.6	
Saving/credit union	25.7	34.4	78.6	38.3	
Home	5.7	9.4	7.1	7.4	
Relatives and friends	8.6	0	0	3.7	
Mean amount of savings	2107.74	718.81	214.11	1302.36	F statistics=6.92; between group df= 2; within group df = 63

SOURCE: Own survey

As can be seen from Table 4.7, saving/credit unions (38.3 per cent) and 'equib'[6] (37 per cent) are the two most important institutions where the poor save. 'Equib' lies outside the protective regulation of the law. Despite this, it forms an important livelihood strategy for the bulk of the poor. Banks (13.6 per cent) are not important institutions for the poor households. Though 'equib' cannot substitute banks, credit unions provide comparable service to that of a bank. Credit unions' capacity, however, depends on the financial resources contributed by the members. As the financial capacity of the poor forming credit unions is usually weak, the services derived from the same will not be adequate.

The importance of the place of saving varies by type of towns. 'Equib' is less important in Addis Ababa compared to the secondary towns and small towns (see Fig. 9). Credit unions, on the other hand, are important in Addis Ababa as opposed to other towns. The fact that 'equib' is less important in Addis Ababa shows that the poor in Addis Ababa rely less on social network for purposes of savings in contrast to those in small towns.

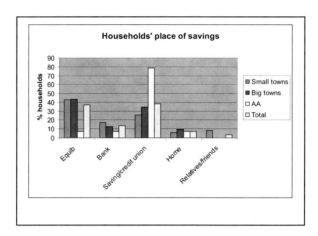

Figure 9. Households' place of savings

SOURCE: Own source

Nearly half (50 per cent) of those who saved reported that they did not get any interest from their saving. These are people who use '*equib*' or keep their money in their home or with relatives and friends. The fact that they do not get interest signifies that the poor do not really benefit from saving schemes that generate income in the form of interest.

Household expense (53.8 per cent) and investment in business (21.8 per cent) were found to be the two most important purposes of saving (Table 4.8). The fact that over half of the poor use their saving for consumption shows that there is little use of savings by the poor for the generation of income. The third important use of saving is for building/maintaining houses (10.3 per cent). This could be considered as an effort of the poor to build assets since houses are the most important assets of the urban poor.

As can be inferred from Table 4.8, as far as use of savings across towns is concerned, the predominant use in all towns is for household expense. The proportion of households using saving for household consumption is 54.5 per cent in small towns, 45.2 per cent in big towns, and 71.4 per cent in Addis Ababa. Investment in businesses is the second most important use for households in small towns (18.2 per cent) and big towns (32.3 per cent). In Addis Ababa, however, the second important use of saving is for maintaining/buying house (14.3 per cent). The fact that housing has emerged as second most important use of saving in Addis Ababa shows its importance compared to other places where access to housing is not as severe. Though there is some difference in the use of savings among towns, the difference, as shown in the values of the chi-square, is not statistically significant.

Table 4.8 Distribution of use of savings by households (%)

	Small towns	Big towns	AA	Total
Household expense	54.5	45.2	71.4	53.8
Medical expense	0	0	7.1	1.3
Children school	3.0	3.2	0.0	2.6
Buy/built house	12.1	6.5	14.3	10.3
Invest in business	18.2	32.3	7.1	21.8
Mixed use 1	0	9.7	0	3.8
Mixed use 2	3.0	3.2	0	2.6
Mixed use 3	9.0			3.9
		Chi-square value = 19.236, df=18		

SOURCE: Own survey

Note:

Mixed use 1=household expense, medical fee, school fee, build/maintain house
Mixed use 2= household expense, school fee and investment in business
Mixed use 3=household expense, built/maintain house, investment in business

4.1.2.2 Credit

Access to credit does not seem to form a prominent feature in the livelihood of the poor. It is only 29 households or 6 per cent of the total households who reported borrowing in the three months prior to the date of the interview.

Of those who reported borrowing, 54 per cent borrowed from organizations while 45 per cent borrowed from persons. Among lending organizations, micro finance institutions seem to be the most important source of credit. This is mentioned by about 50 per cent of those who borrowed from organizations. About 25 per cent of those who borrowed from organizations got credit from NGOs. On the other hand, government and credit unions are insignificant organizational sources of credit for the poor.

Among those who borrowed from persons, friends (29.4 per cent), family members and relatives (23.6 per cent), shopkeepers (17.6 per cent) and neighbours (17.6 per cent) are the most important sources.

It therefore seems that micro finance and personal borrowing are the major sources of credit for the poor. Though the latter is an informal source, its importance in people's livelihood for those who use it needs to be understood. Informal sources, however, are not reliable and could not provide adequate credit. Besides, their arrangement is not standard and depends on the agreement between the credit provider and credit receiver.

Borrowing is extremely low in Addis Ababa where only two households reported to have taken loan three months prior to the interview. A low figure is also reported in both small and big towns where only 11 households (6 per cent) and 16 households (8 per cent) respectively reported to have taken loans. The proportions of households who took loan in the three groups of towns are not statistically different from each other.[7]

In general, there is less reliance of the poor on credit. The reason why the poor rely less on credit requires further research. It is, however, important to note that those who have borrowed, though very small in number, seem to use the credit productively to generate income. About 50 per cent mentioned that they have invested in businesses (see Fig. 10).

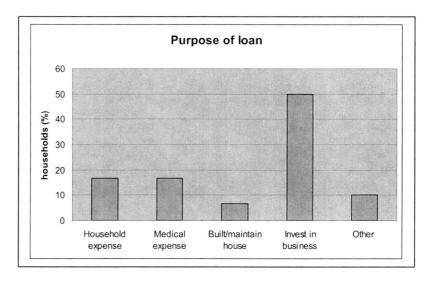

Figure 10. Purpose of Loan

SOURCE: Own survey

The use of credit for productive purpose by households signifies that credit has to be encouraged and possible reasons for the limited use of credit by the poor need to be known. The possible reason for the less reliance of the poor on credit to support their livelihood could be lack of credit availability that meets the conditions of the poor. For example, in urban areas, micro finances require group collateral or membership of an association for the purpose of starting up businesses. Those who are not members or who cannot form a group cannot get access to credit. There has to be an innovative way of addressing the credit needs of urban dwellers by micro finance institutions and others.

4.1.3 Human Assets

Labour is an important human asset for poor people (Moser 1998). It refers to both the quantity and quality of labour resources. It is linked to human capital which represents skills, knowledge, ability to work, and health.

In terms of the quantity of labour force available, age distribution data shows that in all towns the majority are adults who can join the labour force (Table 4.9). On average, nearly two-third of the sample population is adult with no statistical difference among towns. The presence of many adult members in the family indicates that the poor have abundant working labour force. But it has to be clear that the poor also use children as sources of income. In fact, in a focus group discussion it was indicated that the asset base of the poor includes children and own labour. It was mentioned that in urban areas, children bring income to the family since they work as shoeshine boys and even as daily labourers. This mentality of viewing children as an asset and income earner, however, puts less emphasis on the need to invest on children. Under this circumstance, the poor risk perpetuating poverty from one generation to another (Moser 1996).

Table 4.9 Age distribution, by towns (percentage)

	Small towns	Big towns	A.A	Total
Age				
0-4 (infants)	8.9	7.0	7.0	7.7
5-14 (children)	25.5	24.5	20.7	23.9
15-59 (adult)	63.3	65.1	69.6	65.5
60+ (elderly)	2.3	3.4	2.7	2.9
Chi square value = 28.37; df =24				

SOURCE: Own survey

As indicated above, labour asset is linked to human capital. Lack of human capital affects the ability to secure livelihood in urban labour market (Rakodi 2002b). Education and health form the two most important dimensions of human capital. Education has a substantial poverty reduction impact in urban areas. Bigsten *et al.* (2003) have shown that in urban Ethiopia, education of the household head or wife significantly affects both probabilities of moving out of and falling into poverty. In this regard, it was shown that households whose heads or wives had completed primary education had 12 and 22 per cent, respectively, higher chance of getting out of poverty and 8 and 7 per cent lower probability of falling into poverty. Households where the head or wife had completed primary education had, respectively, a 23 and 18 per cent better chance of remaining non-poor. The education of the household head influences the way the household relates to the labour market and thus the income earning opportunities of the household (Muzzini 2008).

In our study, it is found out that most household heads (59.1 per cent) have some form of education that ranges from reading and writing (18 per cent) to higher level or degree level education (0.6 per cent) (table 4:10). Those who are illiterate, however, are substantial forming 41 per cent of the household heads. Household heads with primary education form 12 per cent while those with junior secondary and secondary level of education form 12 per cent and 14 per cent respectively. Following the findings of Bigsten *et al.* (2003), 41 per cent of the household heads who has primary or higher level of education has a chance to get out of poverty if they are given appropriate opportunities.

Table 4.10 Level of education of household head, by sex

	Females		Males		Total	
Level of education	No.	%	No.	%	No.	%
None	157	59.0	46	20.0	203	40.9
Read and write only	46	17.3	42	18.3	88	17.7
Primary	20	7.5	40	17.4	60	12.1
Junior secondary	22	8.2	37	16.1	59	11.9
Secondary	20	7.5	47	20.4	67	13.5
Diploma	1	0.3	11	4.8	12	2.4
Degree	0	0.0	3	1.3	3	0.6
Others	0	0.0	4	1.7	4	0.8
Total	266	100	230	100	496*	100

SOURCE: Own survey

*Four households have not responded to this question.

As can be inferred from Table 4.10, above, the male-female gap in education is quite striking. Females form the majority of those who have no education. In other words, about 77 of the household heads who have no education are females. Kronid (2001) also found that in urban Ethiopia, 58 per cent of the household heads with no education are female-led. Females' primary and secondary level of educational attainment is also much lower than their male counterparts. The gender bias in education and human capital formation is clearly ascertained by other studies. For example, Muzzini (2008) confirmed that urban poor female heads have on average one year of schooling against an average of four years of schooling for poor male head. This indicates that female-led households can stand to benefit most from education.

The data on educational attainment of household heads in different towns shows that nearly half (47 per cent) household heads in small towns and 45 per cent in big towns have no education. The proportion of households in this group is low (20 per cent) in Addis Ababa (Table 4.11). Those with primary and above educational attainment are of similar proportion in small towns (39 per cent) and 41 per cent in big towns, while the proportion is higher (48 per cent) in Addis Ababa. It appears therefore that the labour force in small and big towns has low human capital in terms of education. Muzzini (2008) reported that there is a significant difference in educational outcome between small/medium towns and major towns. The gap between small/medium towns and major towns is 2-years for both adult males and females (*ibid.*).

Table 4.11. Educational attainment of household heads, by towns

	Small towns	Big towns	AA	Total
None	47.0	44.8	20.0	40.7
Read and write only	14.0	13.7	32.0	17.5
Primary	9.0	15.3	12.0	12.1
Junior secondary	8.0	11.7	19.0	11.6
Senior secondary	14.0	11.7	15.0	13.3
Diploma	5.5	1.0	0.0	2.6
Degree	1.0	1.0	1.0	1.0
Others	1.5	0.5	1.0	1.0
N	200	196	100	496

SOURCE: Own survey

The educational status of household members seems to have a similar pattern with that of household heads' educational status across a range of towns. Among towns, Addis Ababa has less proportion of illiterate persons (11.5 Per cent), compared to small towns (31.0 per cent), and big towns (24.6 per cent) (Table 4.12). On the contrary, Addis Ababa has a higher proportion of households who have attained either junior or senior secondary schools (51 per cent) as opposed to small towns (29.2 per cent) and big towns (39.4 per cent). Those who have a primary level of education are of similar proportion in small towns (23.9 per cent), big towns (23.7 per cent) and Addis Ababa (20.6 per cent). It appears that household members in small towns have relatively low educational attainment while those in Addis Ababa have high levels of education, followed by those in big towns. The difference is statistically significant at 95 level of confidence. One possible reason for such difference could be that access to education in small towns is lesser than that of big towns and Addis Ababa. It could also be due to the fact that Addis Ababa and big towns receive more migrants than small towns who are expected to be educated. Alternatively, there is an assumption that households in major cities invest in education more than those in small cities because education has a higher return in major cities (Dubey *et al.* 2001).

On a more general level, the educational status of household members seems to be better than the educational status of household heads. For example it is only 24 per cent of the household members who are illiterate compared to 40 per cent of the household heads. Education of children could be a factor that makes differences in the educational status of household heads and members.

Table 4.12. Educational attainment of household members, by groups of towns

	Small Towns	Big Towns	A.A	Total
None	31.0	24.6	11.5	23.6
Read and write	7.4	5.1	9.7	7.0
Kindergarton	2.3	4.8	4.7	3.9
Primary	23.9	23.7	20.6	23.0
Junior secondary	13.2	18.2	20.8	17.1
Senior secondary	16.0	21.2	30.1	21.6
Diploma	3.8	1.0	1.8	2.2
Degree	1.2	0.7	0.4	0.8
Other	1.2	0.7	0.5	0.8
Chi-square value = 133.08; df= 16				

SOURCE: Own survey

While general education indicates the potential to participate in the labour force, it is the actual skill possession that is an accurate indicator of the potential to earn income. In this regard, it was reported that out of the total 2217 household members, only 226 persons or 10.2 per cent have one skill type. The corresponding proportions for small towns, big towns and Addis Ababa are 9. 4 per cent, 6 per cent, and 7.3 per cent respectively.

These skills are basic skills such as carpentry, masonry, plumbing, etc. Tailoring and carpentry are the two most important skill types in both small and big towns while a mechanical skill, followed by weaving, are the two most important skill types in Addis Ababa. A high level of car ownership in Addis Ababa makes a mechanic's skill to be in high demand. Similarly, a large concentration of population in Addis Ababa also makes a weaving a lucrative skill.

The number of people with two skill types is very insignificant. For example, it is only 25 persons (or 1.1 per cent) who have two skill types. Skill deficiency is therefore a major feature of the poor households in all towns. The majority are forced to earn income from unskilled labour which yields only low and unstable income.

4.1.4 Social Assets

Social assets are derived from membership of a social network. The poor rely on such social assets to derive resources such as information, money, in-kind gifts, etc. These resources enable the poor to withstand the ills of poverty if not rise above them. Social assets minimize risks to livelihood insecurity and mitigate the effects of adverse condition through networks and reciprocity. In general, there is a difference between rural and urban areas in networks and reciprocity and there is a debate in the literature on whether social capital is weaker or stronger in towns and cities than it is in rural areas (Phillips 2002). Box 2 gives typical social networks in urban areas.

Box 2: Examples of social networks in urban areas

Neighborhood-based groupings
Gender and age-based networks and associations
Kinship-based associations (including rural-urban linkages)
Networks based on a common areas of origin
Political-based networks
Religious and ethnic linkages and associations
Savings and credit groups
Employment-based networks and associations (such as trade unions, informal associations, trading networks)
Linkages with NGOs and other external civil society organizations

---

SOURCE: Phillips (2002, 136)

In urban areas, these are more fragile and unpredictable than in rural areas due to fragmentation and heterogeneity of the urban population (Schutte 2004). Moser (1998, 4) indicates that:

> Community and inter-household mechanisms of trust and collaboration can be weakened by greater social and economic heterogeneity, associated with wider distributional ranges of income, opportunities and access to infrastructure, services and political influence in urban areas.

The capacity to respond to changes to external environment depends both on community level trust and collaboration and social cohesion embedded in households and inter-household level relationship (Moser 1998).

In this study, it was found that the support the poor receive from relatives is
not substantial. For example, it was only 13 per cent of the total household
heads who reported to have received some support from relatives (see Fig
11). This does not vary much among towns. Those who received support
form 12.1 per cent, 13.9 per cent and 12.0 per cent in small towns, big
towns, and Addis Ababa, respectively. There is no statistically significant
difference among them. The two towns with the highest support are
Wuchale (24 per cent) and Dessie (20 per cent). The result indicates that
families can not rely on kins and relatives for their need.

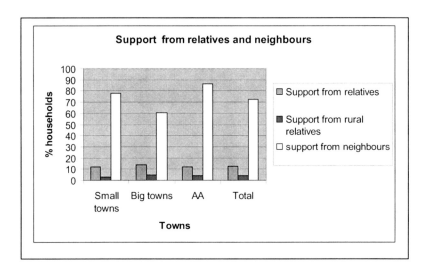

Figure 11. Support from Relatives and Neighbours

For those who received support from kins and relatives, the predominant
type of support has been food support (Figure 12). Nearly half of those who
reported support from relatives mentioned that they receive food support.
This, perhaps, is not surprising given the critical need of food by the poor
(see the section on vulnerability). Other supports which were mentioned by
15 per cent are combinations of food support and other services. Food
support is the predominant one in small towns (54.5 per cent), while it was
46.2 per cent in big towns,, and 60 per cent in Addis Ababa. A combination
of food support and access to services come second in importance among
all towns. The difference among towns in this regard is statistically
insignificant.

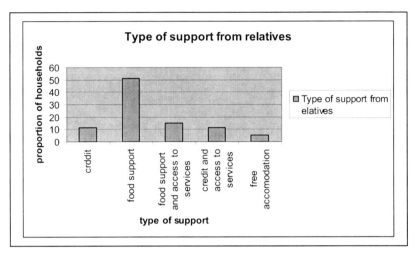

Figure 12. Type of Support from Relatives

Support for the urban poor does not come from rural areas. It is only 4 per cent of the household heads who reported support from their rural relatives. This is also negligible in small towns with only 3 per cent of the households reporting support from rural areas and only 4 per cent in both big towns and Addis Ababa reporting the same. The lack of support from rural areas ascertains the weak rural-urban linkages that exist in Ethiopia (Tegegene 2009). Household relation that could be considered as a mechanism for pooling and sharing consumption (Moser 1998) was found very limited in the study area.

It is, however, interesting to observe that the urban poor rely much more on immediate neighbours. A significant proportion of the household heads belong to neighbourhood associations. About 73 per cent of the household heads belong to neighbourhood associations. Addis Ababa has the highest proportion (86 per cent) of households who reported neighbourhood associations as opposed to those in small towns (78 per cent,) and big towns (61 per cent). The difference in the proportion of households who belong to a neighbourhood association in different towns is statistically significant[8].

The neighbourhood associations can be traditional, such as 'idir', 'ekub', religious associations, or non-traditional. The fact that the majority belong to neighbourhood associations is an indication that there is a substantial amount of neighbourhood cohesion in the urban areas that can be exploited. Information on casual labour market (35.5 per cent) and access to services (19.6 per cent) are the two main types of resources the poor reported to have received from neighbours. The patterns across towns in this regard are similar. Such neighbourhood support is an indication that community support is stronger than an extended family or household relations in urban areas.

4.1.5 Natural Assets

Natural assets in the form of natural resources and the various institutional arrangements that determine access to them are more important in rural areas than in urban areas. In urban areas people use less of natural resources to purse their livelihood. Some of the natural resources that could be of significance in urban context include solid waste materials, river water and common grazing land. Solid waste materials could be considered as assets if the poor utilize them to earn income either through recycling the materials or even simply collecting them for disposal. River water and common grazing land in urban areas could support urban agriculture and improve the livelihood of the poor.

The above observation that natural assets are less important in the urban context is born in this study. It was only 3.9 per cent or 19 households who reported making use of natural resources and recyclable materials in the urban areas. It is interesting to note that no household in Addis Ababa reported the same. Ten of the households who reported making use of waste materials are in small towns while the remaining 9 households are found in big towns. Common grazing areas for sheep and goats and common drinking sources for animals were reported by nearly two-thirds of those utilizing the natural resources.

4.2 The Dimensions of Urban Livelihoods Strategies

Households pursue different types of activities or apply different livelihood strategies in order to earn livelihoods. There are several ways of classifying the livelihood strategies of people. One categorization is between income enhancing, expenditure reducing, collective support and external representation (Farrington et al. 2002). Other categorization includes productive activities and social activities (Schutte 2004). These and other categorizations reveal the variety of activities the poor undertake in pursuing their livelihoods. Such choices affect household livelihood security. The following sub-sections describe the productive activities (income enhancing), expenditure reducing and consumption, social activities, reproductive activities, and collective support mainly based on remittance. The aim is to understand the variety of activities the poor engage in as part of their livelihood.

4.2.1 Productive Activities

Engagement in productive activities is the main form of livelihood strategies in urban areas. The productive activities refer mainly to labour market participation, engagement in entrepreneurial activity or involvement in the informal economy (Beall 2002).

Moser (1998, 4) points out that:

> The highly 'commoditized' nature of the urban sector means that labour is the urban Poor's most important asset, generating income either directly in terms of its monetary exchange value through wage employment or indirectly through the production of goods and services which are sold through informal sector self-employed activities.

The need to get food, health care, education, transport, fuel, etc. constantly put pressure on the poor as they have to get cash to purchase these items. In their attempt to get cash, they engage in various activities, including informal and formal activities. This was ascertained in the focus group discussion. Daily labour, petty trade, local drink and '*Injera*' selling, fuel wood and charcoal vending and sex work were the ones frequently mentioned by most focus groups discussants. It can be understood that the above sources of livelihood are very low paying and marginal activities. Thus it is very difficult to get enough sources of livelihood from such activities. It can also be seen that a good number of occupations mentioned by the focus group members are carried out by women alone. '*Injera*' baking, selling local drinks such as '*tella*' and '*araki*', and sex work are entirely the domains of women. Women also form the majority of those engaged in selling vegetables, onions, etc. in small neighbourhood markets, locally known as 'Gulets'.

The household data on the work status of all those who earn income in the household revealed that casual/piece work is the most important source of livelihood (33.7 per cent) (see Figure 13). However, casual work not only pays small amount in piece rate, but is also very unstable and lies outside the realm of labour law. Those who work as casual labourers face seasonal variance, irregularity and low income.

The second most important type of occupation is employment in self business (23.8 per cent), with 16.6 per cent engaged full time and 7.2 per cent working as part time in own business. This is an indication that the poor, in their attempt to better their lives, engage in small businesses that need to be identified and supported. Full time regular wage employment is used only by 15 per cent. It is presumed that this type of employment ensures predictable wage income and stable working environment. The fact that it has only a small percentage means that the poor are not major beneficiaries of wage income. About 12 per cent get their livelihood from part-time wage employment. This shows the irregularity of the sources of livelihood.

The work status of household members by town groups shows that casual/piece work is dominant in all groups of towns. Those engaged in casual work in small towns, big towns and Addis Ababa are 33.5 per cent, 31.4 per cent, and 37.1 per cent respectively. Nearly one-third or more derive their income from this source. Addis Ababa has the highest casual/piece work. The second most important source of income is full time self employment for both small towns and big towns, while in Addis Ababa the second important work status is full-time wage employment. The fact that wage income comes second in importance in Addis Ababa supports the idea that wage income is an important source of income in major towns (Muzzine 2008). This is confirmed by the fact that both full time and part-time wage employment are reported by 27.7 per cent in small towns as opposed to 31.4per cent in big towns though part-time wage is very low in Addis Ababa. The difference among towns is statistically significant (Chi square value = 143.31 and df =20).

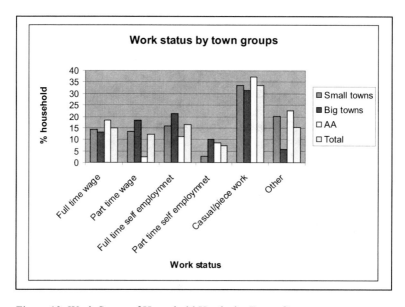

Figure 13. Work Status of Household Heads, by Town Groups

The pattern of work status among household heads is given in table 4:13. Out of 496 household heads, 396 or 80 per cent earn income. Household heads engaged in casual work are the majority forming 35.4 per cent and are followed by self employment (28.2 per cent) and wage employment (24.5 per cent). Employment status of the head of the household by sex revealed that 43.3 per cent of the female heads are engaged in casual/piece work while the corresponding figure for male heads is 26.2 per cent. This is indicative of the fact that women in their attempt to earn income are faced with difficulty emanating from casual work. Wage employment is higher for males (36.1per cent) as opposed to females (14 per cent). One possible reason could be that wage employment requires some kind of education which is not attained by females. Table 4:10 revealed that 59 per cent of females has no education.

Table 4.13. Work status of household heads by sex

Work status	Male	Female	Total
Full time waged	19.1	9.1	13.9
Part time waged	17.0	4.8	10.6
Casual/piece work	26.2	43.3	35.4
Full time self business	22.3	17.8	19.9
Part time for self business	5.9	10.6	8.3
Unpaid family work in family business	0.5	1.4	1.0
Commission seller	1.1	0.5	0.8
Not working for money	3.7	7.7	5.8
Pension	0.5	0.0	0.3
Others	3.2	4.8	4.0
Total	100	100	100
N	188	208	396

SOURCE: Own survey

Employment status was found to have close relation with level of education. As Table 4.14 shows, out of the 140 household heads engaged in casual/piece work, the majority (41 per cent) are illiterate. Similarly, among the 79 households engaged in full-time own businesses, 38 per cent are illiterate. On the other hand, out of 55 employees in full-time wage work only 20 per cent are illiterate, while out of 42 employees in part-time wage only 19 per cent are illiterate. Moreover, those with senior secondary and above educational qualification are found in greater in number in waged employment compared to those in self businesses and casual work. It thus seems that wage employment requires high level of education while literacy matters less in casual work and own businesses. At the same time, one of the reasons for the Poor's lack of access to wage employment is due to lack of education.

Table 4.14 Major employment status of household heads, by level of education

	Full-time wage	Part-time wage	Casual/piec e work	Full-time self business	Part-time self business
None	20.0	19.0	40.7	37.9	27.3
	(11)*	(8)	(57)	(30)	(9)
Read and write	18.2	11.9	17.8	16.4	27.3
	(10)	(5)	(25)	(13)	(9)

Primary	10.9	11.9	17.1	12.6	9.1
	(6)	(5)	(24)	(10)	(3)
Junior	12.7	11.9	14.2	12.6	27.3
Secondary	(7)	(5)	(20)	(10)	(9)
Senior	29.0	19.0	10.0	17.7	9.1
secondary	(16)	(8)	(14)	(14)	(3)
Diploma	5.4	19.0	0	1.3	0
	(3)	(8)	(0)	(1)	(0)
Degree	3.6	2.3	0	0	0
	(2)	(1)	(0)	(0)	(0)
Others	0.0	4.7	0	1.3	0
	(0)	(2)	(0)	(1)	(0)
Total	55	42	140	79	33

*Numbers in parenthesis represent reporting households

SOURCE: Own survey

4.2.1.1 Wage/casual Work

The average monthly payment for those who are engaged in wage or casual work four weeks prior to the date of the survey was 317.57 birr. This is just about the poverty line of US $ 1 per day or slightly less given the prevailing exchange rates. There is no statistically significant difference in the monthly earning of those engaged in wage and casual work among towns. In small towns the monthly earning is 315 birr while monthly earning in big towns and Addis Ababa is at 307 and 338 birr respectively. Those who are paid per week get an average income of 59.32 birr while those who receive daily payments on average receive about 10 birr (see Table 4. 15).

It was only 20 individuals who reported in-kind payments, and 10 individuals who reported bonuses or tips in the preceding 4. For practical reasons, these payments do not make difference in the monthly, weekly or daily income of individuals.

Table 4.15. Monthly, weekly and daily earnings of wage and casual work

	Small towns	Big towns	A.A	Total	F-values
Monthly payment	314.6	307.8	338.8	317.5	F=0.202 Between group df=2 Within group=364
Weekly payment	78.04	57.57	41.74	59.32	F=0.811 Between group, df =2 Within group df=105
Daily payment	9.83	10.23	10.72	10.30	F=0.123 Between group, df=2 Within group, df=191

4.2.1.2 Self Employment- Own Account Work

About 24 per cent of the total or 183 individuals reported that they earn income from own business, employed either as full-time or part-time. Of these, 152 individuals reported the kind of businesses they are engaged in. The main types of business are selling food, selling clothes, and selling household and personal items (see Table 4.16). Those engaged in wood or metal work, transport and construction are relatively less in number. The possible reason could be that these require special skills and some capital, both of which could be in short supply among the poor. The businesses are operated at low level, and there is no major difference among towns in this regard.

Table 4.16. Distribution of businesses pursued by self-employed people, by number of respondents

	Small Towns	Big Towns	Addis Ababa	Total
Selling food	16	36	11	63
Household items and personal items	6	10	4	20
Selling clothes and related items	6	27	6	39
Repair	1	2	0	3
Tailoring	4	3	0	7
Metal /wood work	2	4	0	6
Hairdressing	0	3	0	3
Butchery	1	0	0	1

Selling wood/charcoal	0	2	0	2
Transport/construction	3	4	1	8
Total	39	81	22	152

SOURCE: Own survey

Regarding business operation sites, the majority (33.1 Per cent) reported that they operate their businesses in house. As such, most of the poor are engaged in house-based activity. Others (22.7 per cent) operate in market areas. Those who are engaged in petty trade need to go to the market area to sell their items. The remaining (22.1 per cent) reported that they are mobile and operate in different locations of the city while 21.4 work in fixed location in the town or the city (Table 4.17).

Table 4.17. Business operation sites

	Small Towns	Big Towns	A.A	Total
In house/on plot	28.6	27.2	70.0	33.1
Fixed location elsewhere in the city	23.8	19.6	25.0	21.4
Market area	19.0	28.3	5.0	22.7
Variable location	28.6	23.9	0.0	22.1
Others	0.0	1.1	0.0	0.6
Chi-square value=20.125; df=8				

SOURCE: Own survey

The most important business operation site in Addis Ababa is in-house (70 per cent). In small towns, mobile operation and in-house operations each accounted for 29 per cent while in big towns businesses operate in market areas (28.3 per cent) and in-house (27.2 per cent).

The use of a house as a business operation site by the majority indicates two points. First, most of the businesses are home-based businesses. These include selling of food mainly 'injera',[9] local drinks, tea, etc. Second, it signifies the importance of a house as an asset for income generation for the poor households. This falls in line with the observation made by Moser (1998) that in the urban context housing is an important asset that generates income through the use of its space for home-based production activities.

The businesses operated by the poor are not only run in the house but are mainly self-run. It was only 19 individuals[10] who reported hiring paid workers while another 22 individuals[11] are assisted by family [members]. One of the reasons for self-running the businesses could be the smallness of the business and lack of capacity to hire workers.

Only 45 individuals or nearly one-third of those engaged in own businesses were willing to disclose their annual sales. The rest were disinclined or mentioned that they did not recollect their sales amount. The average amount of annual sales for those who reported is 2988.80 birr. This is about 250 birr per month. Since this is their total sale, it does not clearly indicate their income. It is, however, possible to assume that, on average, their monthly income is less than the specified amount. The annual sales in the different towns are 3251.47 birr, 889.87 birr and 3806.47 birr in small towns, big towns and Addis Ababa respectively.

About 48.2 per cent of the households reported that their businesses have gone down in the last twelve months while 41.8 per cent reported no change (Table 4.18). It was only 10 per cent who reported improvements in their business. Businesses which are not prospering will not have a potential to support the poor. One of the reasons for this could be lack of re-investment in the business. For example, 82 per cent of the respondents mentioned that the first important use of the income from the business is for food and household expenditure, and only 11 per cent said they re-invest in the business (see Fig 14). This is an instance of depleting the business and could be a reason for the loss of income.

With respect to groups of towns, the majority of households in Addis Ababa (75 per cent) and in big towns (52 per cent) mentioned that their businesses had deteriorated. In small towns, 60 per cent indicated that there was no change in their business operation (Table 4.18). In all cases, there are scanty evidences that businesses are growing. And as it is known, a stagnant or a declining business has a low chance of surviving.

Table 4.18. Trends in prospects of business operation

	Small towns	Big towns	A.A	Total
Business is growing	9.5	9.6	12.5	9.9
Business is declining	31.0	51.8	75.0	48.2
Business remained the same	59.5	38.6	12.5	41.8
N	42	83	16	141
Chi-square value =11.96; df=4				

SOURCE: Own survey

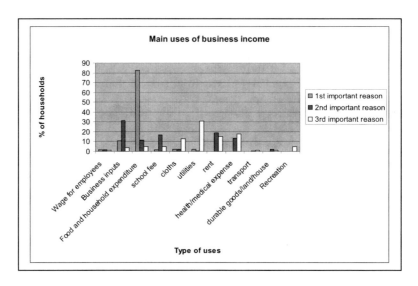

Figure 14. Main Uses of Income from Business

4.2.1.3 Farming and Livestock Raising

Urban and rural agriculture could be important sources of livelihood for the poor. Many studies have indicated that the poor engage in urban agriculture mainly to cater for own need and also for raising income. The poor also engage in livestock breeding as a source of income. Small ruminants could also be important sources of income as they can easily be disposed of. Similarly, the insatiable urban demand for milk and dairy products provide opportunity for the poor to raise cows in the city and derive income from the sales of dairy products. In fact, in some cities, this is an important source of income. For example in Nakuru town in Kenya, three-quarter of the urban households are engaged in agricultural activities located either in rural or urban areas (Owuor 2006).

In this study, farming was reported by 21 heads of households out of the 468 households who responded to this question. This represents only 4.5 per cent of the total respondents. This finding is similar to the one reported by Muzzini (2008) who mentioned that only 7 per cent of the urban population rely on urban agriculture. It is interesting to note here that 20 of the household heads are from small towns, and only one from big town and none from Addis Ababa. The 20 households form 20 per cent of the total sample from small towns. This shows that, first, it is quite clear that farming is not a major activity for the majority of the respondents. In the study sample, therefore, both urban and rural agricultures do not figure in the livelihood strategy of the poor. Second, the fact that those who reported farming were only from small towns clearly shows that in relative terms, farming offers an opportunity in small towns. For the 20 per cent of the households in small towns farming occupies an important position, and thus it has more potential in small towns compared to bigger towns. The fact that small towns are closer to rural areas could be one reason for some households in small towns to engage in farming. Households in these small towns have acquired land through acquisition from *kebeles* (10 households), inheritance (8 households) and lease (2 households).

Livestock possession in the study areas seems to repeat the patterns of farming. First, livestock possession was reported by a few households. It was only 37 households (or 7.7 per cent) of the total households who reported possession of livestock for generating income.[12] Second, the distribution is highly biased in favour of small towns. Out of the 37 households, 27 households (or 75 per cent) were from small towns. These, specifically, were: Welenchiti (14 households), Asendabo (6 households), Wuchale (4 households), and Merawi (3 households) who reported possession of livestock. The remaining 10 household heads (25 per cent) are found in big towns and none in Addis Ababa. Fourteen households reported possession of sheep and another 14 households, cattle. Sheep are used for quick disposal while cattle are held longer for milk and milk products. Both of these are highly demanded in urban areas.

4.2.2 Transfers- Remittance, Food aid and Gifts

The poor in urban areas are likely to benefit from transfers. Transfers come in different forms, such as remittance, food aid, gift, pension, etc. In this study, 50 household heads (or 10 per cent) of the total households have reported receiving transfers (Table 4.19). This is much lower than what is reported by the Welfare Monitoring Survey and Household Income, Consumption and Expenditure (WMS/HICE) studies. Transfers therefore are not major sources of livelihood for the majority in our study. One of the reasons is that public transfers in Ethiopia are mainly directed to rural areas.

For those households who receive transfers, the three major types of transfers are remittance from abroad (32 per cent), remittance from domestic (26 per cent) and food aid (18 per cent). The first two can be designated as private transfer and the third as public transfer.

Table 4.19 Proportion of households receiving transfers, by type of transfers

	Small towns	Big towns	A.A	Total
Remittance from abroad	39.1	11.1	55.6	32.0
Remittance from domestic	21.7	33.3	22.2	26.0
Food aid and food for work	30.4	11.1	0.0	18.0
Gift	4.3	11.1	22.2	10.0
Pension	4.3	27.8	0.0	12.0
Others	0.0	5.6	0.0	2.0
N	23	18	9	50

Chi-square value=21.947, df=14

Across urban areas, remittances from abroad and domestic sources, which are private transfers, dominate in large towns. In small towns, in addition to private transfer, public transfer in the form of food aid and food for work are important sources of transfers. Muzzini (2008) states that public transfer is higher in small/medium towns than in major towns and Addis Ababa.

Transfers come both in cash and in kind. Out of those who reported to have received transfers, a total of 11 households (8 in small towns and 3 in big towns) acknowledged that they received transfers in kind. On average, a total of 1670 birr per year is received by those who reported transfers on cash. This translates into a monthly payment of 139 birr. Though this is not substantial, it could be a good complimentary source of income. Those in small towns receive higher amount (1888 birr) compared to those in big towns (1593 birr) and Addis Ababa (1232 birr). The average amount of receipts both in cash and in kind are given in table 4.20.

Table 4.20 Average value of receipts from transfers (in birr)

	Small towns	Big towns	A.A	Total	
Average receipt in cash over a year	1888.3	1593.3	1232.0	1670.3	F=0.230 Between group df =2 Within group df = 31
Average value of in-kind receipt over a year	101.05	37.0	0.0	86.2	F=0.364 Between group df =1 Within group = 11

SOURCE: Own survey

4.2.3 Expenditure

The patterns of expenditure indicate how a financial asset is managed and which consumption is given priority over others. It is very difficult to get a reliable estimate of expenditure and income from a small scale survey due to over and under-reporting. At national level, there are estimates of expenditure at rural and urban level for different regions and for the whole country. It can be seen that the per capita expenditures in urban areas for the three study regions are higher than that of rural areas (Table 4.21). This is indicative of the high pressure put on the urban poor since different items necessary for life are purchased in urban areas, requiring a high level of expenditure. In the absence of micro data, the regional data on expenditure could be used as a proxy for the amount of income needed to meet the expenses. Consequently, if the poor households in this study are to maintain the regional averages, they require a household income of 6136.7 birr in Amhara region per year (urban per capita expenditure weighted by average urban family size in the region),[13] 7411.1 birr in Oromiya region, and 9471.6 birr in Addis Ababa. It can be seen that households in Addis Ababa require a much higher income. This could be a manifestation of the higher cost of living reflected in per capita expenditure and also of a higher family size than Amhara and Oromiya regions.

The national and regional data show that the proportion of non-food expenditure in urban Ethiopia is 65 per cent of the total expenditure. In the three study regions, Amhara, Oromiya and Addis Ababa, the proportion of non-food expenditure is 66 per cent, 64 per cent, and 67 per cent respectively. Non-food expenditure in rural Ethiopia is 51 per cent of the total expenditure. Household expenses for house rent, electricity, water, etc. in urban areas are the main items that raise the amount of non-food expenditure.

Table 4.21-. Distribution of per capita expenditure 2004/05, by regions

	Rural					Urban				Grand Total	
	Total	Food	Non food	Total	Food	Non food	Total	Food		Food	Non-food
Amhara	1076.7	506.7	569.9	1658.57	571.33	1087.25	1131.63	512.86			618.77
Oromiya	1157.55	582.27	575.28	1764.57	634.37	1130.21	1219.41	587.58			631.83
Addis Ababa	1732.74	721.25	1011.49	2202.70	728.97	1473.73	2197.01	728.88			1468.13
National	1147.47	561.39	586.06	1908.95	671.84	1237.11	1255.54	577.07			678.47

SOURCE: WMS (2004/05)

In addition to the level of expenditure, it is worth looking at consumption patterns in order to understand the situation and livelihood of the poor. In terms of food consumption, the study has inquired the food basket of households of the month prior to the study. As can be seen in Figure 15, cereals (59 per cent), pulses (93 per cent), spices (85 per cent), and wheat (44 per cent) were reported to have been purchased in the preceding month by a relatively higher proportion of households. Other food types, such as milk and milk products (13 per cent), meat and meat products (19.5 per cent), and fruits (15 per cent) are consumed by a fewer proportion of the households. This shows that the majority of the poor follow a strategy of consuming less costly food though the nutritional value of these products could be poor.

Consumption of food across urban spectrum shows that cereals, pulses, spices and wheat are the major food items of consumption. Wheat products, such as macaroni and spaghetti are consumed highly in Addis Ababa. The consumption of meat, milk and milk products, and vegetables, though low compared to other food items, was reported by higher proportion of households in small towns compared to big towns and Addis Ababa. One possible factor for this could be that some households in small towns have their own livestock which could be used as sources of animal products.

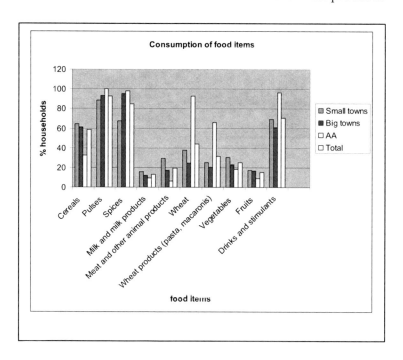

Figure 15. Households' Consumption of Food Items, by Towns

In terms of non-food items consumption, the majority of households reported spending for water (87 per cent), electricity (79 per cent), '*iddir*' (68 per cent), house rent (65 per cent), and household items (51 per cent) (Figure 16). Though not in the majority, a relatively high proportion also reported that they had expended for purchase of used cloth (33 per cent), education (31 per cent), cooking fuel (kerosene) (29 per cent), and medical purposes (20 per cent). These items thus form the foremost expenses incurred by the majority. The poor then are under pressure to meet these expenses.

The pattern of expenditure across urban areas shows some differences as well as similarities. In all towns, three expenditure items, namely electricity, water and '*iddir*' payments were reported by more than 50 per cent of the households. In big towns it was 73.2 per cent, and in Addis Ababa, 86.0 per cent. However, house rent in Addis Ababa has figured as the principal expenditure item but was not so in small towns. In addition, kerosene was mentioned by 76 per cent of the households in Addis Ababa. This indicates the heavy reliance of households in Addis Ababa on gas supply for fuel while this is not the case in small and big towns.

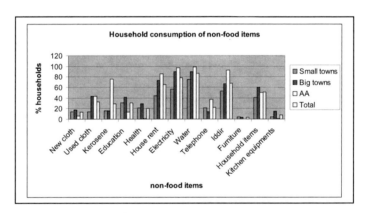

Figure 16. Households' Consumption of Non-food Items, by Towns

The above trend denotes that the poor have a high expenditure needs. In order to meet their expenditure needs and cope with their livelihood, one of the strategies the poor follow is reducing their expenditure. In this regard, this study found that cutting food expenses is one such a strategy. This is done either by purchasing poor quality food (14.4 per cent), purchasing less amount of food (13.3 per cent) or both (19.5 per cent) (see Table 4.22). The strategy is indicative of the fact that the urban poor suffer from hidden hunger. Hidden hunger results from a diet comprised of cheap food and insufficient intake of micronutrients and vitamins (Schutte 2004). Hidden hunger results in health problems and ultimate death in both children and adults.

Some households, in addition to reducing food expenses, also reduce transport cost (2.7 per cent) and health expenses (4.1per cent). In the case of the former, the poor are forced to walk and in the case of the latter they are forced to avoid visiting health centres. A combination of strategies involving reduction of food, medical and transport costs is reported by many households.

The coping strategies across the towns show that in small towns the strategies focus more on reducing food expenditure either by purchasing less food or poor quality food, or both. The reduction of transport cost, together with that of food expenditure, seems to be common in big towns and Addis Ababa. There is a statistically significant difference in the coping strategies among the towns as revealed in the results of the chi-square test.

Table 4.22. Coping strategies of households, by group of towns

	Small Towns	Big Towns	A.A	Total
Walking to work to cut transport cost	1.0	4.5	2.0	2.7
Purchasing poor quality of food	29.8	5.6	2.0	14.4
Purchasing less amount of food	23.6	6.6	7.1	13.3
Not visiting medical facilities	6.8	3.5	0.0	4.1
Walk to work and purchase poor quality of food	0.0	9.1	4.1	4.5
Walk to work and purchase less amount of food	0.5	4.0	51.0	12.1
Poorer and less amount of food	33.0	13.6	5.1	19.5
Walk to work, poor quality and less amount of food	2.6	17.2	16.3	11.3
Walk to work, poor quality, less food and no medical visits	0.5	20.2	0.0	8.4
Poor quality, less food, and no medical visits	0.0	8.6	4.1	4.3
Other	2.2	7.1	8.3	5.4
N	191	198	98	487
	Chi-square value = 441.204, df= 38			

SOURCE: Own survey

4.2.4 Social Activities

Social activities underlie social assets and could be important elements of livelihood security especially for the poor. Social relations serve as social security for the poor in the absence of formal social security system. Maintenance of social relations is thus one type of activities to be pursued.

As Table 4.23 shows, there is a strong evidence regarding social network. This is manifested in terms of visiting friends, neighbours and relatives, and attending various social events. The fact that the majority of households mentioned that they engage in such activities shows the value they attach to social networking. In fact, 83.3 per cent of the households mentioned that they visit their neighbours and 81 per cent responded positively to the question whether they attend social events. Nearly two-thirds of the households also mentioned visiting their friends and relatives. The variation among towns is not significant and almost the same pattern is repeated. In terms of time investment, neighbours are visited regularly by 46 per cent of the respondents, and this is also true of in Addis Ababa (87.2 per cent) and big towns (43.7 per cent). Even in small towns, neighbours are the ones which are visited regularly more than others. This corresponds with the above findings on social asset which ascertained neighbourhood association to be more important than relations with relatives and kin groups. Such investment of time is a manifestation of the importance of social relation in the community. The poor therefore draw on their social networks through their social activities. At this junction, it is important to note that the poor form network not only with other poor but also with rich households as well. In this way, the poor can get access to resources that can supplement their income and improve their livelihoods.

Table 4. 23. Proportion of household reporting social activities*

	Small Towns	Big Towns	A.A	Total
Visiting relatives	83.7	39.1	85.4	65.6
Visiting neighbours	92.9	71.0	90.6	83.3
Visiting friends	88.1	55.7	46.9	66.5
Attending life cycle activities (birthday, wedding, funeral etc)	87.7	64.9	97.9	80.8

SOURCE: Own survey

*Note: Questions are worded in a 'yes' or 'no' format.

Table 4.24. Proportion of households reporting frequency of visits*

	Small Towns		Big Towns		A.A		Total	
	Regular visit	Sometimes visit	Regular visit	Sometimes visit	Regular visit	Sometimes visit	Regular visit	Sometimes visit
Relatives	5.1	62.9	10.5	18.6	4.8	31.0	7.2	39.0
Neighbours	29.1	58.2	43.7	21.3	87.2	12.8	46.0	34.2
Friends	5.5	74.0	33.1	20.0	14.3	60.7	18.3	49.9
Life cycle events	15.9	40.0	12.4	21.5	2.2	18.3	11.8	28.5

*Note: those who responded that they visit rarely or never visit are not shown in the table

SOURCE: Own survey

4.2.5 Reproductive Activities

Various activities are undertaken by households for maintenance and reproduction. These include cooking, washing, cleaning, firewood collection, fetching water, etc., which are fundamental to a household's well being, and thus are invariably undertaken by all households. The majority of the households indicated that these activities are overwhelmingly carried out by females. Ninety-six to ninety-seven per cent of the households agree that child rearing, cooking and cleaning activities are performed by females (see Table 4.25). Though water fetching is still dominated by females, there is some participation of males in this activity as reported by 23 per cent of the households. There was little or no variation among towns in this regard. The average age of all those who participate in reproductive activities shows that all of them are adults (36-40 years of age) (Table 4.26), which indicates that child labour is not heavily involved in reproductive activities of households.

Table 4.25. Gender composition of household members participating in reproductive activities

	Small Towns		Big Towns		A.A		Total	
	Male	Fem.	Male	Fem.	Male	Fem.	Male	Fem.
Cooking	3.6	96. 4	2.1	97.9	2.0	98.0	2.7	97.3
Cleaning	6.8	93.2	1.6	98. 4	4.1	95.9	4.2	95.8
Fetching water	19.1	80.9	19.2	80.8	31.1	68.9	22.9	77.1
Child rearing	3.2	96.8	2.7	97.3	2. 4	97.6	2.9	97.1

SOURCE: Own survey

Table 4.26 Mean age of persons participating in reproductive activities

	Small towns	Big towns	A.A	Total
Cooking	38.2	40.3	41.1	39.6
Cleaning	35.8	38.5	38.1	37.3
Fetching water	34.1	37.5	34.6	35.6
Child rearing	37.9	38.6	34.0	37. 4

SOURCE: Own survey

Though reproductive activities are undervalued, they underlie all other activities. In fact it is mentioned that patterns of people's productive work (i.e. income generating) cannot be understood without considering their reproductive activities (Shutte 2004). The link could easily be seen since below-standard reproductive activities can affect households' assets such as health and the individual's capacity to generate income. There is, therefore, a need for reproductive labour force. Households which cannot hire such labour force will be forced to assign the head, spouse or children to perform such activities. This will withdraw labour force from income generating activities, or asset building activities such as education.

4.2.6 Vulnerability

Vulnerability refers to insecurity of the well-being of individuals, households, or communities in the face of a changing environment (Moser 1996). The environmental changes can be ecological, economic, social or political, and can be in the form of sudden shocks, long-term trends or seasonal cycles (*ibid.*). Vulnerability indicates the probability of falling into or deeper into poverty due to exposure to external economic shocks and stresses (Wratten 1995; Rakodi 2002b). As such, it is able to capture the process of change as people move in and out of poverty.

The analysis of vulnerability involves both the threat and the resilience or the responses to the threats. The means of resistance are the assets that individuals and households possess and their capability of mobilizing them. Moser (1996) formulated the Asset Vulnerability Framework and stated that vulnerability is closely related to asset ownership. Households with more assets are less vulnerable while those with less assets are more vulnerable. At the household or individual level, the ability to avoid or reduce vulnerabilities depends also on the households' ability to transform assets into income, food or other basic necessities effectively (*ibid.*).

In this study households' exposure to shocks and risky events was identified, and the most frequently occurring event was found to be food shortage, comprising about 44 per cent of the total events (Table 4.27). In urban areas availability of food at household level depends on levels of cash income and changing food prices. Food security is an important issue and it depends on the ability of an individual or a household to render its endowments into an effective command over food via direct access or exchange relations, through mobilizing resources from social network or through state support or humanitarian assistance (Schutte 2004). Such entitlements, however, are very difficult in urban Ethiopia because of low income or income loss, absence of state-derived entitlements, and limited or no assistance derived from NGOs.

Tegegne Gebre-Egziabher

Table 4. 27 Frequency and percentage of households who faced events, by sex

	Male		Female		Total	
	Frequency	Percentage	Frequency	Percentage	Frequency	Per cent of Total Events
Food shortage/insecurity	67	41.6	77	46.4	144	44.0
Ill health	32	19.8	33	19.8	65	19.8
Complete loss of income	16	9.9	16	9.6	32	9.7
Eviction from rented house	10	6.2	11	6.6	21	6.4
Intra-household conflict	8	4.9	4	2.4	12	3.6
Inter-household conflict	7	4.3	1	0.6	8	2.4
Death of family member	7	4.3	8	4.8	15	4.5
Illness or death of livestock	8	4.9	3	1.8	11	3.3
Loss of regular employment	2	1.2	5	3.0	7	2.1
Eviction from occupied land	1	0.6	4	2.4	5	1.5
Eviction from charity house	1	0.6	2	1.2	3	0.9
Death of breadwinner	0	0.0	2	1.2	2	0.6
Marriage or engagement	2	1.2	0	0.0	2	0.6
Total	161	100	166	100	327	100

SOURCE: Own survey

The second most frequent event experienced is ill health (20 Per cent). Temporary ill health or chronic illness affects livelihood strategies and makes households vulnerable. Health risks are enhanced more by poor housing, lack of sanitary facilities, and lack of access to basic needs and facilities. In this study, it has been noted that the poor have inadequate housing and no access to waste disposal. These can therefore be important causes of ill health. In terms of basic needs, though access to clean water is somewhat adequate, it is not only its availability that matters to the health of human beings, but also its protection and use. The poor in general have limited materials and capability to use water in a safe and appropriate manner. Some NGOs have realized such problems and included a programme of distributing water containers to poor households in order to help them keep the water clean once it is ready for use at home. Ill health in general requires medical treatment which adds pressure on the already low household income especially if there is a need for a constant medical care.

Loss of income (10 per cent), and eviction from rented houses (6.4 per cent) were also reported as the third and fourth important events respectively. Loss of income is a serious risk to urban households as it implies lack of access to basic necessities: housing, food, health care, transport, and the like. This study, as was discussed above, found that most people rely on casual wage labour. These jobs are irregular, unreliable, and seasonal, and do not yield secure sources of income. As a result, the poor are highly vulnerable to loss of income. This creates its own pressure since the poor have at least to buy food and pay rent. Lack of inability to pay rent usually results in eviction from rented houses as reported by 6.4 per cent of the households. Those evicted from rented houses will have their livelihood seriously compromised since housing provides basic protection.

Other shocks experienced by households include: death of livestock (3.3 per cent), death of family member (4.3 per cent) and conflict within household (3.6 per cent).

The patterns of shocks do not seem to vary by gender. The dominant shocks, which are food shortage, ill health, loss of income and eviction from rented house, are felt in the same proportion among males and females.

The events or shocks, however, show clear differences across urban spectrum. First, households in Addis Ababa reported much lower shocks or events (only 14 individuals reported shocks). By contrast, many households both in small towns and big towns have faced varieties of shocks (see Table 4.28). Second, food shortage is the principal shock in big towns and small towns. Ill health is experienced by a higher proportion of households in small towns, compared to big towns. Small towns are therefore highly susceptible to human asset vulnerability.

Table 4.28 Frequency and percentage of households who faced events, by town groups

	Small Towns		Big Towns		Addis Ababa		Total	
	Frequency		Frequency		Frequency			
Food shortage/insecurity	47	34.8	91	51.1	6	42.8	144	44.0
Ill health	41	30.3	22	12.3	2	14.2	65	19.8
Complete loss of income	12	8.8	20	11.2	0	0	32	9.7
Eviction from rented house	12	8.8	9	5.1	0	0	21	6.4
Intra-household conflict	2	1.5	8	4.5	2	14.2	12	3.6
Inter-household conflict	3	2.2	5	2.8	0	0	8	2.4
Death of family member	7	5.2	7	3.9	1	7.1	15	4.5
Illness or death of livestock	9	6.6	2	1.1	0	0	11	3.3
Loss of regular employment	1	0.7	4	2.2	2	14.2	7	2.1
Eviction from occupied land	0	0	4	2.2	1	7.1	5	1.5
Eviction from charity house	0	0	3	1.6	0	0	3	0.9
Death of breadwinner	0	0	2	1.1	0	0	2	0.6
Marriage or engagement	1	0.7	1	0.5	0	0	2	0.6
Total	135		178		14		327	100

SOURCE: Own survey

In terms of asset vulnerability, it was possible to identify different asset vulnerabilities on the basis of the response from households. In general, the reported events correspond to human, physical, financial and social assets.. For instance, ill health depletes human assets as health is an important aspect of human capital. Food shortage also affects the health of people, thereby deteriorating their human capital. As housing is a single most important physical asset of the poor, the reported events such as eviction from house and land put the physical asset in danger. Similarly, the event of livestock illness or death is a deterioration of physical assets. Loss of income and regular employment are an indication of financial asset vulnerability while events of conflicts both within and across households endanger the social assets of the poor. The mapping of events into asset vulnerabilities indicates vulnerability to poverty is found in household endowments and shows the mechanisms that facilitate deprivation [which] becomes harmful.

In this study, it is shown that human asset vulnerability is the most frequently occurring event, followed by physical asset vulnerability and financial asset vulnerability (Table 4.29).

Table 4.29 Mapping of events into asset vulnerability

Asset Vulnerability	Outcome
Human asset	Ill health, food shortage
Physical asset	Eviction from rented house, eviction from occupied land; eviction from charity house; death or illness of livestock
Financial asset	Loss of income, loss of regular employment, death of bread winner,
Social asset	Inter and intra household conflict; marriage or engagement

SOURCE: Own survey

Households devise different ways of coping with shocks and risky events they face. As mentioned earlier, food shortage is the major type of risk households faced, and thus one of their coping strategies in this regard was decreasing food consumption. This is done by eating less amount of food and skipping meals. Some households have reported that they take food only once a day, mainly dinner, and skip both breakfast and lunch. The other strategy is to purchase less amount of food or cheaper and/or poorer quality of food in order to make up for the food shortage. The implication of taking poorer and lesser amount of food has also been discuused earlier. It results in poor health and malnutrition leading to hidden hunger. Relatives and neighbours are also asked for help particularly for food in order to make up for the deficit. As was indicated in the preceding section, the major form of support the poor receive from relatives is food support. Mobilizing social support is therefore a mechanism to overcome food shortage. Households also indicated that they sell their commodity and goods or work additional hours in order to earn income and purchase food. The former means that food insecurity leads to a widespread depletion of assets (Schutte 2004), while the latter implies that the poor should spend all their time on work in order to purchase food. Table 4:30 illustrates the various ways the urban poor try to cope with the risks and events they face.

The coping strategies employed for ill health include visiting health centres, using traditional medicine, seeking free service and assistance from NGOs, and staying in bed. Free medical services are obtained with a support letter from *kebeles*. In fact, one of the assistances the poor mentioned in a Focus Group Discussion was getting a letter of support to get medical assistance mainly from government offices.

Table 4.30. Distribution of coping strategies reported by households

Type of Risk	Coping Strategy
Food shortage/insecurity	Decrease food consumption (eat less food, skip meals);buy less and poor quality of food; seek assistance from neighbours and relatives to get food; sell commodity and goods; work additional time
Ill health	Visit health centre; use traditional medicine; search for free service; seek assistance from NGOs; stay in bed
Complete loss of income	Borrow money; look for additional work; pray
Eviction from rented house	Seek assistance from *kebele* to get house replacement; borrow money to pay overdue rent; Change house
Inter and Intra-household conflict	Seek arbitration from neighbours; seek arbitration from *kebele*; go to legal courts; resolve within the house
Death of family member	Assistance from '*idir*'; assisted (being consoled) by neighbours and community
Illness or death of livestock	Seek other way to support life; do nothing
Loss of regular employment	Search for other work; beg
Eviction from occupied land	Go to the courts; Go to the *kebele*
Eviction from charity house	Negotiate with those responsible
Death of bread winner	Join relatives or neighbours to live with
Marriage or engagement	Reduce expenses

SOURCE: Own survey

Borrowing money and looking for additional work are steps followed to overcome loss of income and employment. Borrowing obviously puts households in debt, and especially if they cannot repay the loan this is an additional pressure. In extreme cases, people resort to begging and praying when desperation sets in. Seeking assistance from *kebele* is followed as the main coping strategy for shocks related to housing and eviction from land. This is understandable since the *kebeles*, the closest government unit for households, have the capacity to alleviate these problems. The FGDs, however, have shown that such assistance was not forthcoming from *kebeles*. Reliance on social network is also an important means of coping strategy particularly in cases of death and social conflict. The neighbours through their '*idir*' console families faced with death, and are also helpful in resolving both intra and inter-household conflicts. This is consistent with the findings reported earlier that neighbours' social network is an important aspect of social capital in urban areas.

4.2.7 Wealth and Well-being

One indicator of livelihood outcome is the state of wealth and well-being achieved by the poor as a result of the livelihood strategies they follow. As can be inferred from the Figure below, first, the majority have classified themselves then and five years before as being the poorest households or poorer than most households in the community. Second, the number of those households who classified themselves as the poorest at the time of the study was found to have increased compared to five years ago This indicates the deepening or the spread of poverty over a wider range of population (Figure 17 shows the perception of the poor regarding their state of well-being at that point and five years earlier).

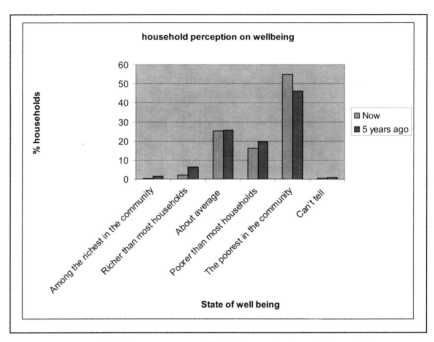

Figure 17. Households' Assessment of Their Economic Status Then and 5 years
        Before

As far as households in different towns are concerned, those who classified themselves as the poorest has risen very sharply in Addis Ababa compared to other towns. As shown in Table 4.31, the proportion of households who classified themselves as 'the poorest' has increased from 5 per cent to 49 per cent in a period of five years in Addis Ababa. As shown above, households in Addis Ababa have low assets and high expenditure, and these situations could be contributing factors for the deepening of poverty in Addis Ababa.

The number of households who classified themselves as the poorest, however, was much higher in small towns than in big towns and Addis Ababa, both at present and five years ago. This indicates the relative position of households within each town.

Table 4.31. Households' perception on their well-being then and five years before, by town groups

Perception	Small Town		Big Town		A.A		Total	
	Now	Five years ago	Now	Five years ago	Now	Five years ago	Now	Five years ago
Among the richest in the community	0.0	1.0	1.0	2.0	0.0	2.0	0.2	1.6
Richer than most households	1.5	1.5	2.5	4.0	3.0	21.0	2.2	6.4
About average	18.5	14.6	28.4	32.0	32.3	34.0	25.2	25.5
Poorer than most households	18.5	19.2	14.9	11.1	15.2	38.0	16.4	19.7
The poorest in the community	61.0	62.1	52.2	50.5	48.5	5.0	55.0	46.0
Can't tell	0.5	1.5	1.0	0.5	0.0	0.0	0.6	0.8
N	200	200	200	200	100	100	500	500

Well-being difference 5 years ago – chi-square value= 136.6; df=14
Well-being difference at present-chi square value =44.1; df=14

The welfare position of households was also examined in terms of income, food and clothing adequacy (Figure 18). In terms of income, an overwhelming majority (85 per cent) indicated that the income they got in the last one month was not adequate to cover their expenditure need. The proportion of people who mentioned the same was much higher in some cities like Merawi (100 per cent), Bahrdar (100 per cent), Adama (98 per cent), Wuchale (92 per cent), and Wulenchiti (90 per cent). Though there is variation among cities, on average 86 per cent reported that they had also experienced food insufficiency in the preceding one month. The figure shows that there is almost a one-to-one correspondence between inadequacy of income and inadequacy of food. This is due to the fact that in urban areas people have to purchase food, and as a result, their income status determines their food acquisition/consumption status. Similarly, clothing shortage was reported by a greater proportion (81 per cent), and this also shows a very close relationship with household income. Some variations in food and clothing adequacy status were also noted among cities.

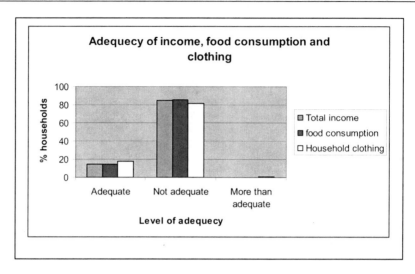

Figure 18. Adequacy of Income, Food Consumption and Clothing, by Percentage

Households indicated that their levels of income and food consumption have shown a worsening situation compared to some years ago. In terms of income, the majority (55 per cent) of households have also indicated that their income now was worse than their income five years ago, while in terms of food consumption about two-thirds or 63 per cent indicated that their consumption of the same food type had decreased compared to two years ago.

The foregoing facts show that the welfare position of the poor is not only very low but is also getting worse increasingly.

4.3 Summary on Asset Status and Livelihoods of Households

It has been indicated that assets form the core of household strategies. The above discussion examined the status of the five types of assets across households in small towns, big towns and Addis Ababa. The following summarizes the main observations along the five types of assets.

1. Possession of productive assets is not a common phenomenon among the sample households. In particular the poor do not seem to possess tools and equipments and livestock resources which could be used to generate income. About one-fifth of the households reported possession of housing as an asset. A majority or four-fifth do not own a house, which is an important asset in urban areas.

    Households in small towns are better endowed with livestock resources and house asset. Houses in small towns are, however, poorly provided with housing and community facilities. If properly planned, these two types of productive assets could be capitalized as a hedge against poverty for households in small towns. Endowment with non-productive resources is very negligible among all groups of households.

2. Saving and credit activities of households in general indicate that financial assets are limited among the study groups. This is reflected in low rates of savings and borrowing across all groups of households. Households in small towns appear to have a higher amount of saving than those in big towns and Addis Ababa. This could be taken as indication that households in small towns earn a relatively higher income than those in big towns and Addis Ababa. The meagre savings are primarily used for non-productive household expenses, while the meagre borrowing, in contrast, seems to be directed mainly to productive use. Credit therefore could be used as instrument to generate income for the poor.

3. There are many adults in poor households. Labour force availability is thus a major endowment of households. The quality of labour force, however, is poor. A substantial proportion of household heads have no education. This is more pronounced in small towns. Similarly, skill deficiency is a major problem of the labour force. The majority (90 per cent) across the different town groups do not have skills. Unskilled labour tends to generate low income that may not be sufficient to meet needs.

4. Neighbourhood associations and support from neighbours are main forms of social relations and assets across all towns groups. Households in all town categories rely less on relatives and kin for social support.

5. Natural resource assets are not widely used. Very few individuals benefit from waste materials, common grazing land and water resources. This is true for all towns groups.

The above points underscore that urban households in Ethiopia suffer from lack of assets. In situations where asset possession is minimal or do not exist, the possibility for the poor to become vulnerable to and not resist shocks is high. It is quite possible to discern some differential in asset possession among the groups of towns. The poor in small and big towns are not equally endowed with respect to livestock, housing and education. Households in small towns fare better in their livestock and house possession but fall short in the quality of their labour force. Assets which are commonly available across a range of towns are labour force and higher neighbourhood associations. On the other hand, savings and credit are found limited in all groups of households across of the study towns.

In terms of livelihood, casual/piece work is the dominant form of productive activity for most of the households. This is followed by self business in big towns and by wage employment in Addis Ababa. For those engaged in self business, houses are the main business sites, indicating the importance of home-based activities. In all towns, businesses are run by owners, indicating the lack of capacity to hire workers. Income derived from the businesses is low, with businesses showing no signs of prosperity. Gender and education differences are also observed along the productive activities though the variations across towns in this regard are minimal. In other words, sources of livelihood across towns are by and large similar.

Though urban farming and livestock raising are not major sources of livelihood for all households, they have higher importance in small towns than in big towns. Similarly, transfers have not figured prominently in the livelihood of the poor.

The lack of income and low levels of welfare have prompted the poor to adopt various expenditure reduction strategies. Among these are cutting on food, reducing transport cost, and health expenses.

The study in this regard has also found that social and reproductive activities are carried out side by side with productive activities. These activities are important as they provide support for productive activities and livelihood.

Shocks and events are experienced by households in general. Food shortage, ill health, low income and house eviction are the major shocks households reported. Events or shocks vary by town groups. While a few households experience shocks in Addis Ababa, the number of households who experienced shocks in small and big towns is higher. By the same token, households' coping strategies are found to vary depending on the nature of the shocks experienced.

CHAPTER 5

THE EXISTING POLICIES, PROGRAMMES AND INSTITUTIONS OF URBAN POVERTY REDUCTIONS

Policies and institutional contexts are critical in livelihoods since it is these contexts that either block and disable or encourage and enable livelihood (Ellis 2000). The policy and institutions context provides insight into the different poverty reduction strategies pursued at macro and meso level. Macro level pro-poor policy, urban development policy and urban governance are the major aspects of the current urban poverty reduction strategies. The following sections will describe these policies and programmes so as to form the background for the next chapter which attempts to see the link between the livelihood requirements and existing policies. This chapter does not examine the impacts of these interventions on the beneficiaries of the programme as this is beyond the scope of the present study.

5.1 Pro-poor Urban Policies and Programmes

5.1.1. PASDEP and Urban Development Policy

The wide-spread nature of poverty in Ethiopia is very obvious. This is manifested in a number of dimensions. According to a government source, in 2005 about 31 million people were living below poverty line, earning equivalent to USD 0.45 cents a day, and between 6 and 13 million people are at risk of starvation each year (MoFED 2006). This indicates the depth and severity of income poverty. The non-income dimension of poverty is also as severe or as worse as income poverty. For example, in 2004/05 more than 15 per cent of children died before their fifth birthday; 47 per cent were malnourished; maternal mortality rate was at 871 per 100,000; 48 million people did not have access to clean water, and only 17 per cent of the population had electricity (*ibid.*).

In light of the magnitude of the problem, the Ethiopian Government embarked on the Poverty Reduction Strategy Papers (PRSPs) in 2000/01. It issued the first phase of the PRSP process under the Sustainable Development and Poverty Reduction Programme (SDPRP) which covered the period 2000/01-2004/05. PASDEP is the second phase of the PRSP process extending for the period 2005/06-2009/10. PASDEP focuses on growth in order to finance the necessary social investment in human development and to break out of the self-perpetuating poverty traps (MoFED 2006). In addition, massive scaling up of efforts to reach the MDGs for Ethiopia through intensified sectoral programmes, such as education, health, and water supply is envisaged as the second prong of the poverty reduction strategy (*ibid.*).

PASDEP has set targets for overall growth to be achieved by the year 2009/10, including in the areas of agriculture, education, health, infrastructure, finance, etc. There are eight strategies envisaged in order to achieve these targets. These are:

- Massive push to accelerate growth;
- Geographically differentiated strategy;
- Addressing the population challenge;
- Unleashing the potential of Ethiopia's women;
- Strengthening the infrastructure backbone;
- Managing risk and volatility;
- Scaling up to reach the MDGs; and
- Creating jobs.

PASDEP outlines sectoral policies, programmes and targets. Agriculture, food security and vulnerability, private sector, export, tourism, mining, infrastructure, health and education have specific programmes and targets. Cross-cutting sectors, namely gender, children, population, HIV/AIDS, environment, capacity building, governance and decentralization, youth and employment were also dealt with.

Though all the strategies are important for rural and urban areas, particularly those related to urbanization agenda, rural urban linkages, infrastructure and employment creation, and urban development have explicit emphasis on the urban sector. In terms of urban development, the strategy indicates that there is a need to focus on urban poverty and welfare as much as on enhancing the contribution of urban centres for national development (MoFED 2006). It is clearly stated that the main objective during the PASDEP period is to achieve the goals of the national urban development policy.

Urban development policy in Ethiopia has come late compared to the heavy emphasis given to rural policies and strategies. It was only in 2005 that the government realized the importance of urban centres in the overall development of the country in general and in rural development in particular. The government's attention on urban development was thus made explicit in the PASDEP strategy (*ibid.* 49) where it was stated:

> It is recognized that there will inevitably be a growing trend towards greater urbanization and that a significant part of the modern sector growth will inevitably take place in urban areas. Furthermore, hundreds of small towns represent tremendously important future growth poles. Without sacrificing the historical

emphasis on rural population, under PASDEP, the government will intensify efforts in the urban sector.

An explicit manifestation of the above intention was the formulation of the National Urban Development Policy which was approved by the Council of Ministers in 2005.

The main trust of the policy is that "Ethiopian cities provide efficient and effective public services to residents, compliment and facilitate rural development, are models of participatory democracy and build accelerated economic opportunities that create jobs" (*ibid.*)

The national urban development policy has two main packages: i) the urban development package; and ii) the urban good governance package. The urban development package answers the question on 'what' the government is going to do in the next four years in terms of service delivery of urban based public services: jobs, houses, roads, schools, clinics, water supply, etc. The urban good governance package answers the question on 'how' the government will deliver the public services of the urban development package which are described in terms of efficiency, effectiveness, accountability, transparency, participation, sustainability, the rule of law and security (MWUD 2007). The two programmes define the government's 'urban agenda' for the implementation of PASDEP.

The objectives of the urban development package are to reduce unemployment and poverty, to improve the capacity of the construction industry, to alleviate the existing housing problems, to promote urban areas as engines of economic growth and to improve urban social and economic infrastructure particularly for the youth. The package has five pillars: micro/small enterprise development programme, integrated housing development programme, youth development programme, provision of land, infrastructure, services and facilities, and rural urban and urban-urban linkages. It also has eight goals which are related to the five pillars (see Table 5.1).

The urban good governance package includes land development and administration system improvement, urban planning improvement, public participation, urban infrastructure and service improvement, justice reforms, organization and human resource management reform, urban finance and financial management reform.

Table 5.1 Goals of the urban development package

Goal 1	Construction of 400, 000 houses in 72 urban centres during EFY 2006/07 to 2009/10. Twenty to thirty per cent of the beneficiaries will be women.
Goal 2	Create employment opportunities for 1.5 million urban residents in 825 urban centres during EFY 2006/07-2009/10. Fifty per cent of the beneficiaries will be women.
Goal 3	Enable the voluntary creation of 100,000 small enterprises on a sustainable bases in the construction industry.
Goal 4	Provide social facilities (8250 classrooms, 1030 libraries, 503 youth centres, 7236 football fields, and 503 hand/basketball fields) for youth to gain knowledge and engage in recreation in a productive and meaningful way. Fifty per cent of benefiting youths will be girls.
Goal 5	Ensure the participation of urban residents, public authorities and other stakeholders in all programmes.
Goal 6	Secure funds that provide for a total investment during EFY 2006/07 to 2009/10 of EB 23.3 billion. EB 15.8 billion for the integrated housing development programme, EB 6.2 billion for the micro and small enterprise development programme and EB 1.3 for the Youth programme.
Goal 7	Ensure delivery of a total of 13,825 hectares of serviced land in all urban centres: 1700 hectares to support the integrated housing development programme (IHDP); 4900 hectares for micro and small enterprise development; 1425 hectares for youth development programme; and 5,800 hectares for other development.
Goal 8	Secure funds for the EFY 2006/07 budget in foreign currency equivalent to USD 73.9 million.

SOURCE: Urban PASDEP (unpublished)

Out of the five pillars of the urban development packages, the Micro and Small enterprises (MSE) programme, the Integrated Housing programme, and the Land and Infrastructure Provision have direct impact on poverty reduction.

The MSE programme of the national urban development policy aims at creating opportunities for 1.5 million residents through establishment of one-stop service centres, MSE extension workers, provision of premise and loan, business development services, promoting market opportunities and market linkages and equipping enterprises with modern equipment and machineries (MoWUD 2007). The 1.5 million beneficiaries will be the existing MSE operators/entrepreneurs, MSE operators/entrepreneurs involved in the integrated housing development programme, new technical vocational and educational training programme graduates and the unemployed youth (*ibid.*).

The Integrated Housing Development programme is a low-cost government-sponsored multi-storeyed house construction. The programme has multiple objectives, which include provision of housing, reduction of slum dwellings, reduction of urban unemployment and poverty, enhancement of the capacity of the construction industry, and so on. During the PASDEP years (2006-2010), the programme, among other things, aims to construct 400,000 houses, create 200,000 jobs and promote 10,000 small enterprises (MoWUD 2008). By the year 2010, the programme will have run in 72 medium and large cities of the country. To date, there is no systematic assessment of the MSEs and housing strategy.

5.1.2 City Level Urban Poverty Reduction Programmes and Strategies

The basic guiding principle for city level strategies and programme to reduce urban poverty is the national urban development policy, particularly the Urban Development Package. As indicated above, the package has five pillars: micro and small enterprise, integrated housing development programme, youth development programme, development of land, infrastructure and services, and rural-urban and urban-urban linkages. The three pillars, namely the micro and small enterprises, the integrated housing programme and land delivery are those which are widely applied in almost all cities and towns by municipalities.

5.1.2.1 Micro and Small Enterprises[14]

In all study sites the major involvement of the municipality in poverty reduction is the micro and small enterprise strategy. This is true in both big and small cities.

Micro and Small Enterprises in Small Towns

All the small towns in this study have an MSE strategy. The basic objective in all towns is to reduce urban unemployment and poverty. For small cities, the *woreda* micro and small enterprise agency, the municipality, the *kebeles* and micro finance institutions are involved in MSE programmes. The main institution responsible for this activity is the *woreda* MSE office that is established in different years in different towns[15]. In some towns like Welenchiti, the office has seen some transformation since its establishment. The following are some elements of the strategy and its implementation.

Target groups

The main target groups of the strategy are the unemployed people in the town. These people are required to produce letters from *kebeles* that confirm their unemployed status. In some towns, this requires proof of residency in the town as well. The main target groups qualify for the full package of the assistance. The second target groups are existing businesses in the town. The support package provided to this group is different from that provided for the main target groups.

Implementation modality

The basic implementation modality is that the MSE office organizes the unemployed and forms an association of unemployed people. The number of members of the association has to be ten or more. Priority is given for technical and vocational educational training (TVET) graduates followed by 10th and 12th grade completes and dropouts. Associations are formed because of the belief that it will be easier and effective to provide assistance to associations instead of extending the same to individuals. Resource limitations also necessitate assistance to be provided to associations rather than to individuals. Once the association is formed, training is provided on different subjects like entrepreneurship, savings, and the like. Business plans are also prepared in consultation with the members. One of the major supports provided by the MSE agency is to help the associations get bank loan and saving account. The amount of loan provided depends on the business plan. In addition to the loan, the office approaches the municipality, which is responsible for land allocation in the town, in order to secure land for the associations. Training, land and registration are freely provided for the associations. Besides, the associations are exempted from tax for one year.

In addition to forming and supporting MSE associations, the MSE office also supports individual business people in the town by providing information and consultancy. The office, however, does not extend support to enable them secure loan or land.

Type and nature of work

The MSE office is responsible for identifying the type of activities based on local conditions. It is possible to identify the broader and narrower range of activities that are targeted for support. In broader terms, the work categories comprise industry, trade, services, construction and urban agriculture. In the narrower sense, the types of work identified include textile, metal and wood work, hollow block manufacturing, urban agriculture, municipal service, and food and food products, among others. An important issue in this regard is whether the activities are survival industries or growth industries. Survival industries are those in which the entrepreneur is pushed into. These are activities undertaken to support family income and they could be seasonal or part-time. They require no or low skill and entry barrier is very low. As a result, they are highly overcrowded activities. Earnings from these activities are used to support survival and the enterprises have the potential for making short-term impact on poverty. The growth oriented activities require skills which restrict entry. Entrepreneurs are attracted to the growth-oriented activities by consideration of profits and out of choice. Surplus is re-invested and they form the basis for growth and sustainable development (Harvie 2003).

In the above case, it appears that most of the activities identified do not require skill or need very limited skill. Food and food products, urban agriculture and municipal service are of such types. The others, such as metal work, wood work, and clothing and textile do require skill but the skill requirement is very low. These activities, therefore, have low entry requirement. The chances for these types of activities to be overcrowded in the town are very high. The other feature of the activities is the scale of the activity. The activities are initially supported mainly by loans from micro finance institutions. These loans in general are very low and they limit the scale of the activity.

Achievements and progress

Different levels of achievements and progress have been realized in various towns. These achievements are mostly in the areas of number of associations created, training provided, business plan prepared, and land and loans provided. Though the record keeping systems of MSE offices at *woreda* does not enable us to correctly identify the achievements, there are some indications which highlight that some achievements were made by the respective MSE offices.

At the time of this study, in Asendabo, 8 MSE associations with 82 members were established. About 2000 m^2 of land has been allotted to MSEs in the town. In Welenchiti, a total of 10 MSE associations were formed, with six of them in urban agriculture, three in trade, and one in service. In Merawi, different amount of land has been allocated to the MSEs in different years. A land size of 4978m^2, 30689m^2, 35620m^2 was allocated in the years of 2005, 2006, 2007 respectively, and a total of 397 beneficiaries received land. In Wuchale, 7 associations were created. These are the kinds of achievements reported by different towns. These achievements indicate that efforts are made to realize the goals of MSEs. For instance, about 650 persons were employed in the four towns at the time of the study. Though this could be encouraging, it is not clear how and in what ways this reduces poverty and unemployment on a sustainable basis. Getting some people employed is obviously an important step. The question, however, is that is it possible to form associations of all unemployed people in the town? Can the government provide support on a continuous basis to enable the unemployed start new businesses? Are the businesses feasible and sustainable? A recent study on MSEs in urban Ethiopia indicated that though the MSE programme has some positive impacts in improving the livelihood of beneficiaries, it faces a number of challenges (Tegegne and Meheret 2010). The challenges include the fact that since the programme is based on a huge support and assistance, it has created unrealistic expectations among beneficiaries, that the demand for assistance is getting out of hand and is also leading to a dependency syndrome (*ibid*). This threatens the sustainability and competitiveness of the businesses.

Constraints and problems

MSE strategies in small towns face numerous problems. Some are unique to some towns while others are more structural and apply to all of them. For instance, the fact that the unemployed are required to have ten or more members to form an association has created a major challenge. The main difficulty is that there is a lack of common understanding and agreement among the members of the association, which could be endangering the existence of the association.

The major problems which have been raised during the study by most towns include, inability to get land on time (Merawi, Asendabo), lack of market network (Asendabo, Mreawi), lack of loan, etc. In Welenchiti, defaulting was the major problem which has led the Oromiya Saving and Credit Association to withdraw loan. In 2007, a total of 20,000 birr was provided from the municipality budget in order to compensate for the discontinuation of loan by the Oromiya Savings and Credit. In Merawi, lack of loan was cited as one of the major problems, while in Asendabo, the one-year loan period that applies for working capital was found to be insufficient for repayment.

Micro and Small Enterprises in **Big Towns**

The MSE strategy in big towns, like those in small towns, is derived from the urban development strategy. The objectives of MSEs and the types of activities are similar to that of small towns[16]. In most big cities, the programme focuses on six sectors. These are: textile and clothing, metal and wood work, construction, food and food products, urban agriculture and municipality services. These sectors are believed to be growth-focused sectors. Each association will select the sector in which it wants to participate. There is no limitation as to what number of association should be organized under a given sector.

Institutional arrangements

In the case of big cities, the institutions responsible for implementation of the MSE strategy are city-level micro and small enterprises agency, the city government, the *kebeles* and micro finance institutions. Each of these institutions has specific roles. The *kebele* is responsible for recruiting interested individuals who would like to form an association. There are two kinds of associations. The unemployed will form an association of ten or more individuals while others, including those with some form of employment, can form an association of two or more individuals. The unemployed are expected to bring proof of their status from *kebele* justice committee. The MSE workers ascertain the unemployment status of the applicants. The *kebeles*, in addition to recruiting and organizing the unemployed, will also provide training and prepare business plans for the associations. The city-level agency is responsible for facilitating the necessary inputs such as land, loan, and the like by linking the association with an appropriate institution. Since the provision of land and loan is outside the mandate of the MSE agency, it has no control on such important inputs. Consequently, lack of these inputs delays the associations from starting work. In fact, according to the *kebele* MSE head in Gish Abay *kebele* in Bahir Dar, it can take up to two years for associations to start operation due to absence of readily available land and loan.

Achievements

In Jimma town, the estimated number of unemployed persons was 8000. Of these, job opportunities are created for 3200 people. Out of the total 560 associations, 320 associations have become operational. Those in the industry sector are reported to have shown progress, unlike those in the urban agriculture. One of the major activities accomplished in Jimma town was to create market linkages for the MSEs. For example those MSEs engaged in cleaning are working with Jimma University; others in wood and metal work closely work with condominium houses.

According to the head of the Bahir Dar MSE agency, the agency has created temporary and permanent jobs for 20,000 people starting from 2003. Similarly, over 61 associations have participated in the construction sector. The MSE agency has provided various services related to training, technology, business advice and market linkages. Regarding the latter, it was indicated that the agency had helped 60 associations to take part in business festivals held in the city, and another five associations to participate in a bazaar held in the Sudan.

In Dessie town, where the number of unemployed people is estimated to reach 11,000, the micro and small enterprise development office has helped to establish 282 enterprises with 1613 members. These enterprises are formed by individuals, business organizations or cooperatives. Achievements in Adama are also of similar scale.

Constraints and problems

In all the towns, problems of finance and land are cited as major constraints. In both Bahir Dar and Jimma, studies have identified problems faced by different MSE sectors (The general problems identified are given in Table 5.2). Though there are some specific sectoral problems, the common problems relate to lack of production sites, poor market demand, lack of finance, and lack of competency.

Table 5.2 Problems identified for MSEs in Bahir Dar and Jimma, by sectors

Sector	Problem	Sector	Problem
Tailoring and weaving	-Lack of production site -Lack of marketing area -traditional equipment -poor market demand -poor quality of raw materials -Lack of finance and -Lack of integration between production centre and market condition	Wood and metal sub-sector	-Lack of production sites -Lack of electricity to run the business activity -Lack of competence -Lack of market demand -Lack of finance -Lack of information and -Lack of knowledge about different working regulation and directives related to the sub-sector
Food and food related items	-Sanitation problem -Poor market demand -Lack of competence -Lack of finance and -Shortage of production sites	Urban agriculture	-Lack of focus and negligence of the activity -poor access to production site -Lack of binding laws and regulation and -Lack of knowledge about the benefit of urban agriculture for food security
Construction sub-sector	-Lack of trained entrepreneur -Lack of finance buy construction materials -Lack of knowledge about contract agreement preparation	Tourism	-Lack of access and knowledge about the potential of this sub-sector -Shortage of service giving as well as production sites -Lack of competence -Shortage of finance

SOURCE: FUPI and BMCI (2006) and Oromiya Urban Planning Institute (2008)

In addition, there are some problems specific to different towns. In Jimma, for example, the programme has faced lack of interest by the beneficiaries to form an association; recruitment of employed persons, inadequate provision of land, and unavailability of timely loan from lending agencies. In Adama, it was mentioned that beneficiaries generally prefer government work to engagement in small and micro enterprises. In Bahir Dar, lack of awareness regarding the benefits of associations and the operation of free market are considered as major problems.

Micro and Small Enterprises in **Addis Ababa**

The MSE strategy is a key strategy in all sub-cities and *kebeles* in Addis Ababa. In Addis Ketema Sub-city, MSE activity was started in 2003. At the time of the study the MSE was organized under the Sub-city Industry Development Office which comprises three units. These are cooperatives, MSEs, and regulations. The MSE unit is led by a team leader. At *kebele* level, the MSE is led by a cabinet member, and the MSE team at the sub-city level leads and coordinates *kebele* level MSE activities. The MSE activity at *kebele* level is undertaken by extension workers.

Unemployed youth and women are the main targets of MSEs in Addis Ababa. In addition, some support is also provided to existing enterprise owners who fall within the micro and small enterprises designation. The main responsibilities of MSE units at various levels are the following:

i.) Creation of employment opportunities;

ii.) Preparation of projects;

iii.) Provision of business development services;

iv.) Provision of training (both management and technical training);

v.) Creation of market linkages;

vi.) Facilitation of production and distribution premises;

vii.) Input supply;

viii.) Loan service;

ix.) Advise and consultation; and

x.) Organizing the unemployed youth.

There are five priority sectors of MSE development in Addis Ketema sub-city. These are: textiles and clothing, metal and wood work, food preparation, construction, and municipal service. These priority areas are considered as growth sectors because there is a belief that businesses in these sectors have the potential to grow and expand. They are also labour intensive and it is possible to generate employment in these sectors with limited training and capital.

It is reported that since the beginning of MSE activity in the sub-city in 2003, a number of activities have been accomplished. These relate to forming associations, providing loans, training, production sites, market linkages, etc.

A recent Business Processing Reengineering (BPR) study in Addis Ketema revealed that the existing MSE development programme in the sub-city has problems. These involve the provision of services in a fragmented manner, lack of demand-based assistance, unfair provision of assistance, beneficiary identification problem, weak linkage with stakeholders, and the presence of large scale unemployment in the city and sub-city (Addis Ketema sub city 2009). The BPR study will be used as a basis for a new mode of operation of the MSE development programme in the sub-city.

5.1.2.2 Housing and Residential Land

Housing and land provision are important areas of municipal intervention for poverty reduction. In line with this, Integrated Housing Development is one of the components of the urban development packages. The programme, however, is not operational in small towns.

Small towns

The basic objective of the housing programmes in all small towns is to make land available for those who are able to construct own houses. This involves land preparation by the municipality and allocation through lottery system. Land is allotted for those who can produce letter of confirmation that they had no prior land or house. There is an upfront payment of varying amount for obtaining land. In Asendabo, people pay 500 birr for a 200 m2 plot; in Welenchiti the payment is 2500 birr for same size parcel, while in Wuchale a land size of 100-180m2 requires a down payment of 400 birr. Merawi has a severe land problem because of the difficulty to delineate rural from urban holdings. As a result, land development for housing is found to be problematic.

The strategy of providing land for house construction is an initiative that should be encouraged. But the downside is that, in all cases, first the poor cannot afford to construct a house on their own, and secondly, in some towns the down payment is so high that it is out of the reach of the poor. The alternative is to make *kebele* houses available for the poor. This, however, seems not feasible since almost all existing *kebele* houses are already occupied and there are no new *kebele* houses. It is only very few people who might be able to get *kebele* houses whenever they are vacated.

The poor, due to lack of alternative, in many cases engage in illegally constructing houses or squatting. In Asendabo, for example, it was stated that there were about 600 illegally constructed houses. Though these houses are not yet demolished by the responsible government body, there is an effort to stop any future squatting in the town. In Merawi, the number of illegally constructed houses was reported to be 400 (persona communication with Merawi town manager).

Big towns

Housing shortage is very evident in big towns. According to the head of the Jimma housing agency, there is a 1000 housing deficit in the town. In Bahir Dar, the head of the housing agency stated that about 12,000-13,000 individuals are facing housing shortage. In Addis Ababa, there is a housing backlog of 367,000 units (Yewineshet 2007). In big towns, the housing strategy involves different approaches. These are: Integrated Housing Programme, sometimes called Condominium Housing, land delivery, and *kebele* housing.

Condominium houses are multi-storey houses with different design typologies integrating studios, one-bed room and two-bed room houses. The multi-storey building (usually 2-5 floors) is intended to house 175-300 households per/ha, and the ground floor is used for mixed businesses (*ibid.*). Pre-cast and on-site production of construction technologies that minimize cost and time are used. The approach was first implemented in Addis Ababa on a pilot basis.

Housing agency is established in each city to oversee the construction and management of the condominium houses. The municipality provides land and covers infrastructural cost for the building. The Federal Government facilitates bank loans for regional governments and Addis Ababa to finance the construction. The money will be repaid by collecting from the beneficiaries. The cost of building condominiums involves not only the construction cost but also compensation paid for those displaced in the process of re-claiming land for construction.

The construction of condominium apartments has been underway in all the big towns and the completed projects have also been occupied. According to MoWUD (2008), in Addis Ababa alone, about 33 thousand houses have been built and transferred to beneficiaries since 2004. In other 37 towns, a construction of 61 thousand houses is underway and the building of another 40 thousand houses is being launched in other cities in the year 2008 (MoWUD 2008). According to the head of the housing agency in Bahir Dar, 1655 housing units were constructed in the year 2007. In the same year, 1320 houses were constructed in Dessie and there was a plan to construct 1214 houses in the year 2008. In Jimma 1150 houses were being constructed in 2007. In Addis Ketema sub-city, 1690 houses, out of the total of 2246 houses, are already transferred to beneficiaries.

There is no doubt that the construction of condominium houses will increase the housing stock in each city and at national level. This will help alleviate the housing shortage faced by many cities. The housing shortage, however, is so huge that the construction of condominium will hardly satisfy the demand. For example, the housing agencies in both Jimma and Bahir Dar towns mentioned that there were 5000 people on the waiting list for condominium houses. The other problem is with regard to targeting real beneficiaries. The programme is essentially aimed at low and middle income beneficiaries who will purchase the houses on loan basis with an upfront payment of a certain amount of money. In reality, however, the condominium houses are being transferred to middle and even high-income groups because of its unaffordability to the low-income people. (The specifics regarding the payment and loan arrangements are given in Table 5.3 below).

Table 5.3 Rent and transfer arrangements for condominium houses, by house type

No	Description	Studio	One-bed-room	Two-bed rooms	Three-bed-rooms	Commercial
1	Monthly income average (birr)	300	600	1200	>1800	
2	Average rent (birr)	60	150	300	450	
3	Area (m2)	<20	20-30	30-45	>45	Varies
4	Average price /m2	800	900	1100	1200	Auction
5	Grace period	6 months	3 months	-	-	
6	Advance payment	10%	10%	30%	30%	100%
7	Selling price of house (birr)	16,000	18-27,000	33-50,000	>50,000	Auction
8	Interest rate	-	2%	7.5%	7.5%	
9	Payment period	20 years	10 years	15 years	10 years	
10	Subsidy rate	30%	30%	-	-	

SOURCE: Yewineshet (2007)

As several cities engage in the construction of condominium housing, a range of problems related to the construction have surfaced. In all towns the major problem is shortage of construction materials. In Jimma, for instance, some construction materials have to come from far off places, and this increases the cost of construction. In addition, logistic problems to undertake the work were also cited by the authorities of the housing agency. In Addis Ketema sub-city, key informants mentioned that the condominium projects face problems related to construction quality, site selection and infrastructure. Furthermore, the financial problem of the low-income beneficiaries is creating difficulties in accomplishing smooth transfer of houses.

Land delivery is another form of policy intervention intended to ease the problem of housing in big cities. In Jimma, residential land of 140 m^2 is given on payment bases while land above 140 m^2 is given on lease bases.

The payment for 140 m^2 is 4000 birr. The city government indicated that there were many people who applied for plots and the plan was to distribute land for 2000 people in the year 2008. Though there is no construction regulation, one-third of the 140 m^2 of land should be built up area

In Dessie, residential land is given for cooperatives or individuals. A lottery system is used to allot land for residence. According to the head of the Housing Development Agency, there is quite a substantial demand for residential land. About 289 house co-operatives have been established since 2002, and only forty-nine of them have received land while the remaining are on the waiting list. There was also a plan to give land for 60 cooperatives in the year 2008. At individuals' level, there were 1500 people in the waiting list, and a plan to give land for 500 individuals. The size of residential land given which used to be 00 m^2 is now reduced to 153m^2. The major problem with access to urban land in Dessie town is land shortage which is a result mainly of its topography. Land in the city is composed of steep slopes and hills, and the city also suffers from landslides. These limitations, however, are now overcome by annexing rural areas within 10 km radius. In Bahir Dar, a residential land size of between 100-250 m^2 is provided on payment. Land provision, however, falls much shorter than the demand. For example in the year 2004, there were 10,000 people on the waiting list to get residential land (FUPI and BMCA 2006). One of the consequences of shortage of access to formal land is the proliferation of squatter settlements. In Bahir Dar alone it is estimated that there are 5000 squatter settlements (*Ibid.*). The government attempts to strictly control squatter settlements particularly those constructed after 2004.

5.2 Urban Governance and Decentralization

Governance and decentralization are seen as important elements of poverty alleviation programme of the government. Both SDPRP and PASDEP emphasize the importance of governance and decentralization in poverty reduction.

Ethiopia has undertaken a series of decentralization measures since the early 1990s. First, it carried out decentralization to regions during which time autonomous regional units were created and given space to exercise self-rule. Second, since 2000/01, decentralization to *woredas*, the lowest tiers and administrative units in the country, has been put in place. The latter was aimed at deepening decentralization in the country through empowering local authorities and fostering local self rule and institutional development. These measures are believed to be critical to poverty alleviation by improving accountability, responsibility and flexibility in service delivery and increasing local participation in democratic decision making on factors affecting the livelihood at grassroots (MoFED 2006) The *woreda* decentralization process has necessitated the revision of regional constitutions, deployment of man power from regions and zones, to *woredas,* and establishment of institutions.

Parallel to the *woreda* decentralization activity was an effort to recognize urban administrations as autonomous entities and giving them the right to self-administration (Tegegne 2007)[17]. The Urban Management sub-programme in the context of National Capacity Building Programme (NCBP) was designed to establish a framework for urban administration. The programme focussed on establishing an appropriate framework for municipalities within each region, restructuring and staffing of municipalities, mobilization of financial resources, strengthening of planning and management capacity, and improvement in land management and service delivery (Tegegne 2007). Consequently, beginning from 2002 various regions adopted proclamations to provide for specific government arrangement in urban areas. There were, however, some earlier attempts to recognize municipalities especially by the Oromiya and the Amhara regions[18]. The Oromiya region issued the municipal authorities and rural *kebeles* proclamation number 4/1993 prior to the issuing of the Federal Constitution. The Amhara region has issued two pieces of municipal legislations, namely the Organization of Bahir Dar as a Special Zone and the definition of its duties and responsibilities, Regulation Number 3/1995, and the reorganization of urban *wereda* administration and municipalities, along with the definition of their duties and responsibilities, Regulation 1997 (Tegegne and Kassahun 2004). These legislations, however, were found to be deficient. As a result, and owing to district decentralization, municipalities' proclamations were revised and existing shortcomings corrected.

5.2.1 The Amhara Region

The Amhara region issued a revised proclamation for the establishment, organization and definition of towns in the region in 2003 (Council of ANRS proclamation number 91/2003). Accordingly, cities/towns within the Amhara region are classified into three categories of: City Administrations, Municipal Towns, and Emerging Towns. City administrations are further classified into City Administrations, Amalgamated City Administrations and Metropolitan City Administrations. Likewise, municipal towns are categorized into 'lead municipalities' and 'sub-municipalities' (see Table 5. 4).

Table 5.4 Classification of urban centre in Amhara National Regional State

Urban Centre Category	Sub-classification
City Administration	City administration
	Amalgamated city administration
	Metropolitan city administration
Municipal Towns	Leading municipalities
	Sub-municipalities
Emerging Towns	Communities in transition to be urban centres

SOURCE: Council of ANRS Proclamation no 91/2003

Dessie and Bahir Dar are given a metropolitan city administration status. According to the proclamation, a metropolitan city will be established by more than one city having local administration status on the basis of distinct common relations. Though Dessie is given the metropolitan status, it does not currently fulfil the criteria. The idea is to form a metropolitan city by merging it with other cities and towns such as Combolcah, Tita, Haik, and the like in the future. Similarly Bahir Dar is to combine with it rural *kebeles* such as Deshet, Abraje, Werb, Quaratsionm, Zenzelma and Woramit (Alazar 2008).

In all cases, the rural-urban linkages are poorly developed. In Dessie, though the surrounding areas have been incorporated, the city is not yet capable of providing them with employment opportunities. This will directly put the rural poor in poverty as households have surrendered their land to the City Administrations.

Dessie and Bahir Dar towns are directly accountable to the Regional Council. This gives the towns a zonal status and avoids the interference of zones in their daily affairs. The fact that the towns have zonal status will also enable them to have a wider structure and higher pay scale for the civil servants. The higher pay scale in turn will create incentive for the civil servant to deliver services effectively. In terms of decision-making, the cities through their councils can issue policies and regulations regarding city development. The above specifications are useful to help improve service delivery and local economic development at city level and thereby help reduce poverty.

City administrations have their own organizational structure and distinct mandates of service delivery. In city administration structure, city services are rendered by the Office of City Service. City service includes all urban services[19] except those undertaken by sectoral offices. The office is accountable to the Mayor's Committee and is headed by a general manager.

Financial capacity of cities is critical for service provision and promoting local economic development. The City Governments follow an integrated municipal and state finance. Both municipal and state functions are financed from the same sources and pass through similar financial procedures. It is not, however, clear whether such integrated finance will promote municipal service delivery of the town or not. In an integrated finance, the municipality is treated as one sector and receives its budget from the city administration. The budget allotted to the municipality, however, is not sufficient and does not match the huge service responsibility of the municipality.

The proclamation states that a city administration has a number of financial sources. These include charges and taxes collected from service delivery, block grant from regional government, loan, and other sources. Currently, the main revenue sources for City Administrations are block grant from the Regional Government, service charges, city properties land tax, and et cetera, with block grants forming the major element. The amount of finance available, however, falls short of the expenditure requirements.

City administrations are divided into *kebeles*, which are the lowest administrative units in the city. *Kebeles* have their own organizational structure and distinct mandates of service delivery. They have their own councils and executive committee members. The councils are elected from the residents, and number 400 in Gish Abay *Kebele*. The councils meet every month and listen to the executive committees' reports, evaluate activities and provide guidance to the executive. The Council elects the *Kebele* Administrator from the Council members and the *Kebele* Administrator, in turn, appoints the cabinet members. The appointment of the cabinet members needs to be approved by the Council. The Cabinet members, however, are not necessarily members of *kebele* Council.

Gish Abay *kebele* in Bahir Dar, which is one of the study *kebeles*, has six cabinet members. These are: administrator, deputy administrator, justice head, micro and small scale enterprise head, women's affairs head, and *kebele* manager. The deputy administrator, in addition to its regular assignment, also heads a public relations and social affairs unit. Experts and professionals work under some cabinet members. For example, under the *Kebele* Manager, there are units dealing with land administration, design and construction regulation, urban planning and documentation. Under Finance and Administration, there are units of revenue collection, records, purchase, guards, messengers and cleaners. The justice unit includes militia and regulation units. Each of these has specific role and responsibility. Some cabinet members are appointees, but also operate as experts as well. A case in point is the head of the Women's Affairs.

The *Kebele* Administrator is accountable to the *Kebele* Council and the City Mayor. Other cabinet members have also dual accountabilities. They are answerable to the corresponding office at city level and to the *kebele* administrator. For example, the *Kebele* Manager is accountable both to the *Kebele* Administrator and City Manger. The *kebele* head for micro and small enterprise is accountable to the city head of micro and small enterprises and for the *kebele* administrator. This kind of dual accountability creates confusion among the offices and creates gaps for city agencies to dominate the *kebeles* since city agencies receive priority over *kebele* administrations.

Despite the fact that *kebeles* have such an elaborate structure, their mandates, however, are limited to providing basic and very elementary services. In many cases, *kebeles* are responsible for providing identity cards, birth, death and marriage certificates, letter of support for free medical service, permits for house and fence maintenance, effecting payment for housing allowance, local conflict resolution, overseeing basic infrastructures, such as open drainages, and environmental hygiene, and recruiting and organizing applicants for MSEs.

Though *kebeles* collect revenue from some of these services, the revenue is transferred to the City Administration. For example in the year 2008, Gish Abay *kebele* collected a total of 117,232, birr from the various services it provided to the residents (see Ttable 5.5) and the sum was transferred to the City Administration.

Table 5.5. Amount of revenue collected by Gish Abay *kebele* (2008), by service

Marriage and birth certificate	5,061.00
Market fee	37,592.00
House rent and bicycle plate issuing	58,797.93
Identity card issuing	11,457.00
Engineering services	1,025.00
Penalty fees	1,010.00
Receipts from different government document sale	1,330.00
Service fees	959.44
Total	11, 7232.37

SOURCE: Gish Abay *Kebele* Office

The city administration, in return, allocates budgets to the *kebele*. The allocated budget is used for salaries, covering running costs, and for capital budget. The following Table (Table 5.6) shows the amount of budget requested and allocated to Gish Abay *kebele* for the year 2008.

Table 5.6 Type and amount of requested vis-a-vis allocated budget (2008)

Budget Item	Budget Requested	Budget Allocated
Salary	238,212	237,494
Running cost	110, 279	63,654
Capital budget	56,000	20,000
Total	368,491	321,148

SOURCE: Gish Ababy *Kebele* Office

As the figures in the above table show, the amount of budget received was less than the requested amount by 47,000 birr. Such deficiency entails that the *kebele* has to cancel some of its activities. The *kebele* is more of an implementing and support providing agency rather than an independent and autonomous entity that plans and executes on its own. All the activities carried at *kebele* level are city-level or city wide activities. For instance, in the case of MSEs, the *kebele* is responsible only for organizing applicants and forming associations. The decision for most critical inputs such as provision of land, capital, etc. is made by other agencies though there may be land that can be used by MSEs in the *kebele*. Similarly, in the housing programme, the *kebele* is not entitled to give land for construction. This and similar authorities are not decentralized to *kebele* levels. As a result, some structures in the *kebele* are not functional. A case in point is the land administration section of the *kebele*.

The small towns in Amhara region are classified as either leading municipalities or sub-municipalities. Both Wuchale and Merawi are leading municipalities. They are run by municipal (town) managers who are elected by the *woreda* administration. The towns have town councils comprised of members elected from the residents. In the case of Merawi, at the time of this study, there was a temporary council of 15 members which meets every three months. The Council deliberates on the town development plan, budget and approves the same. In Wuchale, the Town Council has 11 members. The Town Councils are accountable to *Woreda* Councils. The councils, though accountable to the *woreda*, have critical roles in the town. According to the proclamation, the Council is responsible for budgeting, planning and monitoring.

The municipalities lie entirely within the *woreda* administration. In fact, the municipality is seen as one of the different sectors of the *woredas*. The relation between the *woreda* administration and the municipality is that the latter is subordinate to the former. As a result, there are several areas which require the good will of the *woreda* administration. For instance, in Wuchale, the implementation of the decision to incorporate the rural areas surrounding the municipal towns within 2 km (air distance) radius depended entirely on the *woreda* since it is the latter which provided compensation money for the farmers. Similarly, municipalities are not members of the *woreda* cabinet. This isolates the municipality from decision making structure within the *woreda*. Any intervention in the town thus depends on the good will of the *Woreda* Cabinet. The fact that the municipality is not a cabinet member has also affected the pay scale of municipal workers. The municipal workers are paid lower than others. For example, in Wuchale, the municipal manger is paid a monthly salary of 1040 birr while a cabinet member who is head of any given sector is paid 1500 birr per month. This will have its own negative effects on the municipal activities.

In terms of finance, municipalities are expected to raise their own revenue. In both Merawi and Wuchale, however, the finance that can be raised is very small. The main revenue sources in both towns are earning from land sale, livestock tax, and transport tax. In Merawi, the revenue raised in the year 2007 was 282, 678 birr while the expenditure for the same year was 480,181.14 birr. The revenue raised in Wuchale in the same year was 124,628.25 birr with the expenditure level way above the revenue. The amount of revenue collected is significantly lower than the service and the economic requirements of the towns. As a result, municipalities are forced to seek assistance from donors and NGOs or skip service delivery. In many cases, the chances for the municipality to receive assistance from other sources are minimal and if such assistances are available they are not usually sustainable. The financial capacity of municipalities is thus very precarious which limits their service delivery capability. Their technical capacity is even worse than their financial capacity. Most regions have specified their manpower requirements to run the various functions. In reality, however there is a significant discrepancy between the available and the permitted size of manpower. This also constrains service delivery in towns.

Municipal towns are comprised of *kebeles*. Merawi has three *kebeles* while Wuchale has one *kebele*. The *kebeles* are accountable to *woreda* administration politically while they are accountable to municipalities for service delivery. They have dual accountability and this creates confusion with negative impacts on service delivery.

The structure of *kebeles* in small town is quite weak. For example *kebele* 01 of Merawi town does not have elaborate government structure except for the positions of the administrator and the deputy. *Kebele* has 3 support staff, no permanent staff, and no financial support. The *kebele* works only as a collaborating unit with the *woreda* micro and small enterprise office, health office, etc. to implement some activities.

5.2.2 The Oromiya Region

The urban local government proclamation no 65/2003 and the amendment proclamation no 166/2006 are the latest proclamations that determine urban administration in the region. Towns and cities in Oromiya are classified into four grades. Grade one constitutes residents of greater than 90,000; Grade 2 constitutes residents numbering 45,000 to 89,999; Grade 3 constitutes residents from 10,000 to 44,999 residents, and Grade 4 represents residents from 2000 to 9999 (Oromiya Regional Government 2003).

The urban governance model followed in the region is that of the Council-Mayor system. The organs under the City-Mayor system are the City Council, the Mayor, the City Manager and other executive bodies and the City Court. The Council is composed of members elected by city residents on a *kebele* basis. The amendment proclamation limits the Council to First and Second Grade towns only. Thus City Councils are not set up in Grade 3 and 4 towns, and instead, these towns are included under the *Woreda* Council in which they are found. In many 3rd and 4th grade towns there are advisory Councils composed of people from different segments of the population.

Jimma and Adama are Both Grade 1 towns and zonal towns. As First Grade towns, they have own councils and are accountable to the president of the region[20]. Under the City Administration there are both state and municipal functions. The municipal functions are led by the city manager who is an employee and a non-voting member in the Mayor's committee.

Both cities have authority and power to run development functions in the city. Both cities rely on own revenue and subsidy from regional governments. Proclamation no 65/2003 has given power to the local government authorities to introduce new tariff rates, adjust and collect taxes, rentals and service charges in line with federal and regional policies and laws. Table 5.7 shows the amount of revenue collected by five First Grade cities in Oromiya. Within Oromiya, Adama collects the highest amount of revenue, while Jimma ranks third following Bishoftu. The patterns of revenue in both Jimma and Adama, however, show that there is an improvement in their revenue raising capacity.

Table 5.7. Revenue collection of Jimma and Adama vis-à-vis other 1st grade towns in Oromiya, by year (000birr)

	Jimma	Adama	Burrayu	Shashemene	Bishoftu
2003	4,015	11,442.5	-	-	4,105.6
2004	7,674	15,328.2	-	-	11,49.9
2005	8,791	26,874.8	-	-	8,604.5
2006	11,572	40,077.1	2840.6	-	-
2007	10,706.7	15,788.7	-	-	16,146.6
2008	20,050	116,481.6	50,816.9	18,298.6	57,298.6

SOURCE: Oromiya Urban planning institute (2008, 21)

This, however, is not true for all years. For instance, in Jimma though there is positive balance in some years, the revenue cannot meet the expenditure in other years (see Table 5.8)

Table 5.8 Revenue and expenditure of Jimma city (000 birr)

	Revenue	Expenditure
2003	4,015.0	3122.7
2004	7,674.0	6952.1
2005	8,791.0	10514.8
2006	11,572.0	5,591.1
2007	10,706.7	12,832.7
2008	20,050.0	27,470.9

SOURCE: Oromiya Urban planning institute, (2008, 27)

The other feature of towns is the high proportion of recurrent expenditure vis-à-vis capital expenditure. This is quite evident in Jimma. Table 5.9 shows that, except for 2004 and 2005, the recurrent expenditure accounts for more than two-third of the total expenditure in other years. This implies that service delivery is hampered in the city.

Table 5.9 Recurrent and capital expenditure in Jimma city (2003-2007)

	Recurrent	Capital	Total	Recurrent (of total)
2003	2,562.5	560.2	3,122.7	82.1
2004	2,076.9	4875.2	6,952.1	29.8
2005	3510.2	7004.6	10,514.8	33.3
2006	4260.7	1330.3	5,591.0	76.2
2007	8769.9	4062.8	12,832.7	68.34

SOURCE: Oromiya urban planning institute (2008) p.23

Asendabo and Welenchiti towns are Grade 3 towns. In both cases the Mayor is accountable to the *Woreda* Administration and the Zonal Works and Urban Development Office. The Mayor is not a member of *wereda* cabinet. The municipalities are expected to raise their own revenue as they receive no financial assistance from the *woreda*[21]. The towns in general have small revenue.

In 2007, the total amount of revenue collected in Asendabo was 145,000 birr. The major sources of revenue were business tax, tax from house, land allocation, *kebele* house rent, market tax, and so on. The main expenditure items were wages and salaries, support to schools, and capital projects. Because of the limited budget, however, the town could not undertake major development activities. The Mayor of the Asendabo Municipality mentioned that they were not able to pay compensation payment for houses to be demolished according to the master plan, build inner roads in the town and provide entertainment centres for residents. The municipality is attempting to raise its revenue by embarking on new tax sources and raising the tax rates. For instance there was a plan to raise the livestock market tax rate from 2 birr to 3 birr and the fee paid for land was raised from 230 birr to 500 birr.

Welenchiti had relatively a higher income than Asendabo. In 2007 alone, the city government collected 1.2 million birr. Despite this, the municipality is not capable of addressing the major problems of the town. For example according to the town Mayor, the town has a flooding problem which is believed to cost 7 million birr and there is no means of providing this service. The town also does not have standard inner roads and no waste disposal system.

Both towns have not only financial capacity problems, but also face manpower shortages as well. For instance in Asendabo, though the manpower requirement of the municipality was 24 workers, there were only 12 employees at the time of this study.

5.2.3 The Addis Ababa City Government

Addis Ababa is a self-governing chartered city, as established by the Addis Ababa City Government Revised Charter Proclamation 311/2003. It has its own elected Council, a City Cabinet and a Mayor. The Council is elected every five years and is accountable both to the City electoral and the Federal Government. The City Cabinet composed of bureau heads initiates policies and implements proclamations and regulations and policies adopted by City Council and the Federal Government. The Mayor is the Chief Executive Officer and is answerable to the Council and the Federal Government. During the years 2003-2005, the Addis Ababa City Government initiated and completed restructuring and institutional reform that led to the creation of sub-cities. The city is now subdivided into 10 sub-cities and 99 *kebeles*. The sub-cities are responsible for municipal functions within the bounds of their physical space and administer the *kebeles* under them. As already mentioned, the *kebele* is the lowest tier of city administration. It is the centre of communities' involvement and provides some rudimentary services and undertakes regulatory works. Sector bureau offices, agencies and authorities are established at City Government level. They are responsible for implementing infrastructural development, providing economic and social services and executing regulatory services (Addis Ababa City Administration 2009). At sub-city level, there are offices which correspond to bureaus at city level. For example in Addis Ketema sub-city, there are ten offices responsible for education, health, industry, women's affairs, justice, public relations, work and urban development, capacity building and finance. Sub-cities are empowered to plan and execute development activities and identify key focuses of their activity. For example, the Addis Ketema sub-city has identified that integrated housing development, micro and small enterprise development, land and infrastructure development and capacity building as priority concerns.

The Addis Ababa City Government has adequate authority to run the city independently, including the power of issuing and implementing policies concerning the development of the city. It is also empowered to raise revenues and collect taxes, and allocate budgets to sub-cities, which, in turn, distributes down to *kebeles*. As mentioned above, *Kebeles*, as the lowest administrative units in the city, have their own elected councils and executive members. *Kebele* 13/15 in Addis ketema sub-city, for example, has 300 council members and 15 elected executives. Eight of these lead sector units, and the remaining are responsible for political activities in the *kebele*. The sectors represented at *kebele* level are education, MSE, health, capacity building, youth and sport, public relation, and women's affairs. In these sectors the *kebele* is responsible for some level of activities. For example in the education sector, the *kebele* follows up and supports public schools below level two. It does not, however, undertake school construction and maintenance functions. The sector unit heads are accountable both to the *kebele* Chief Executive and sub-city office heads. In case of the need to attend to both officials at the same time, priority will be given to line offices.

In general the *kebele* plays a mobilization and implementation role. Some critical municipal functions that may have significant impact on poverty reductions, such as housing and land, are not within the responsibility of *kebeles*. *Kebeles* therefore have less functional powers than sub-cities. In the *kebeles* included in this study, informants mentioned that the *kebeles* suffered from man power shortages and financial constraints.

5.3 Summary on Policies and Institutions

Policies, urban governance and institutions are critical for livelihood and poverty reduction. They set incentives, facilitate access, and allow space for the inclusion of the poor in decision-making.

In terms of policy, the government has put in place a poverty reduction strategy which recognizes the importance and significance of urban poverty. Though the urban development policy has come late, its acknowledgment of the significance of urban poverty is a step in the right directions. Three main policy areas relate to poverty reduction at city and town level, micro and small-scale enterprises development, and integrated housing programme and provision of land. These three sets of policies are implemented invariably across towns except for the integrated housing programme whose focus is mainly big and medium towns. These policies and programmes, however, have their own implementation problems some of which are town/city specific and others are generic. Their effectiveness and sustainability, at the same time, also need to be investigated.

The new urban governance seems to recognize municipalities, city administrations and sub-cities. These entities are given authority, responsibility and resources. Capacity constraint and resource deficiency, however, are observed in many places. The *kebeles,* which are the lowest administrative unit and closest to the poor, however, have limited power, functions and resources to effectuate poverty alleviation ventures on their own. They only seem to be an implementation agency with rudimentary functions.

CHAPTER 6

LIVELIHOOD REQUIREMENTS, URBAN POVERTY REDUCTION STRATEGIES AND INSTITUTIONS: EXPLORING LINKAGES AND GAPS

6.1 Livelihood Requirements

How poverty is understood determines the way policymakers and planners respond to it. The sustainable livelihood approach provides a unique perspective to understand poverty and provides the basis for intervention strategies designed to alleviate poverty. The following sub-sections explore the insights derived from the livelihood perspective that form the livelihood requirements or interventions to improve livelihoods.

6.1.1 Asset Building Strategies

The role of assets in poverty reduction has been emphasized by several authors. Birdsall and London (1997), for example, in assessing the World Bank poverty reduction strategy, point out that the three-pillar approach to poverty reduction, i.e. economic growth, basic social services to the poor and safety nets, are not adequate. Asset inequality or access of different groups to productive assets (land, education) is found to affect overall growth and income growth of the poor disproportionately (*ibid.*). Empirical studies have also ascertained that ownership of assets plays important role in determining poverty (Sackey 2005). In this regard, Moser (1998) identified the link between asset and vulnerabilities.

The asset status of households in this study was found to be very weak or poor. In other words, they are asset poor households requiring building up of their assets in order to help them lift themselves out of poverty. The four types of assets or capital (physical, human, financial, and social) were found out to be relevant in this study. There is, however, a significant deficiency which needs to be rectified and further enhanced.

Access to Financial Capital

This study revealed that the poor - in both small and big towns - had various expenditure needs. In small towns, people spend more on food and utilities while in large towns they spend on food and rent. On the other hand, in both small and big towns, the poor have very limited saving capacity and do not benefit from loan services. One of the major reasons for low savings was found to be low income. If households do not have enough income, there will be little or no saving. Secondly, if there are no adequate financial services for the poor, i.e. intermediation between the time the poor earn and use income, there will also be no savings. Similarly, the availability of credit and the ability to benefit from credit by producing collaterals or other methods determine the way the poor use loan services.

Improving the income level of the poor is therefore an essential component of strengthening their financial capital. Outside this, however, appropriate financial intermediation or financial services is required to enhance the poor's ability to save and access to loan. For example in terms of savings, the poor use informal financial market in which savings are turned into lump sums. '*Equib*', a rotating saving, is one such mechanism. Informal financial markets, however, have their weaknesses, such as high cost and unreliability. Sometimes the poor will not be able to participate in the informal financial market like '*equib*' which requires the poor to make equal and regular pay-ins as the others (Rutherford, Harper and Grierson 2002). The financial needs of the poor also varies according to their age, marital status, gender, social and ethnic groups, and similar other variables which are not always easily addressed by informal financial services. Under these circumstances, there is a strong argument to support flexible general purpose financial service on a formal or semi-formal basis (*ibid.*).

Similarly there is a need to increase access to institutional credit in order to make the poor benefit from loan facilities. Financial services are required by the poor for a range of reasons, such as common life time needs (birth, death, marriage, widowhood, old age, home building, education, and the like), emergencies (illness, floods, fires, demolishing of squatter settlements), opportunities (to buy assets, to start or run businesses) (*ibid.*). A study in Ghana showed that access to financial capital reduces the risk of households falling below the poverty line by 6 to 9 percentages (Sackey 2005)

Human Capital

Various studies, including Sackey (2005), have shown that that there is a circularity between the human capital asset, and its usage and returns to such investment. The poor have the lowest stock of human capital and receive the lowest rewards. In this study, it has been revealed that there is a relationship between education level and employment in formal wage sector. The ability of the poor to get better jobs is greatly hampered by their low levels of education and skill. The poor in small towns in particular have very limited human capital in the form of education and skills.

Education and training intervention in support of employment should thus be designed to address the shortages of human capital. Rutherford, Harper and Grieson (2002) identified four factors that influence education and training for employment. These are relevance, cost, equity and asset enhancement. These factors have to be properly balanced in relation to local resources and circumstances. In terms of relevance, education should provide the base on which livelihood oriented human capital assets are built and training should respond to the local labour market demand and result in work (employment, self-employment or enterprise). In terms of cost, education should reflect the social and economic returns and training can be made more efficient by cost sharing, making better use of local knowledge and available facilities. In terms of equity, education provision should be made to overcome economic and social barriers and training programmes should accommodate the background and customs of those they serve. In terms of asset enhancement, education should be structured to provide a sound general basis for acquisition of specific work and income-related skills, and training should provide the skills needed to grasp existing work opportunities and to identify future opportunities (*ibid.*).

Raising the educational and skill levels by considering those four factors should therefore be an important intervention in order to build the human capital of the poor and increase their employability and livelihood.

Housing

The major physical capital of the urban poor is house. In this study it was found that house is not only a place for living but also an important area for income generation for the majority. The housing condition of the poor, whether rented or owned, was very poor. In particular, big towns suffer from severe housing shortage that is dominated by poor quality, overcrowded and rental houses. This is a reflection of lack of effective housing policy, housing finance and tenure security in many cities and towns.

Housing the poor is the most challenging aspect of housing policy Many interventions have been made to address the shelter needs of the poor. For example, one intervention was to reduce the entry cost to legal shelter (Payne 2002). This could be done by revising regulatory framework that may entail reducing the entry cots to new land and shelter development. The relaxation of standards for initial plot development will help the low income households to get into the legal housing ladder. In practice, this entails permitting small plot sizes, smaller buildings and basic standards of infrastructure provision. Improvements and extensions can then be financed from future income (*ibid*). It is also important to streamline administrative procedures through one-stop shop or other means, allow mixed use of land and enable the poor to provide rooms for rent or start home-based activities.

The other intervention is assisted self-help. Assisted self-help housing sees the provision of housing for the poor as something the poor should do by themselves in conjunction with the non-governmental agencies, the private sector and cooperatives (Yeboah 2005). The role of the state should be an enabler rather than a direct provider. This line of thinking has evolved into a general policy guideline in housing the poor that advocates plurality (Yeboah 2005). The plurality approach involves a range of providers of house that include the government, the private sector (formal and informal providers), the poor themselves, non-governmental organizations and cooperatives. In order to implement the pluralistic approach there is a need for the government to provide access to serviced land with clean titles and design innovative and targeted finance. This is related to the site and service approach of housing development. The latter will enable the poor acquire access to sewage, bathroom, stand pipes, electricity, etc. and venture into non-conventional building material which are easily accessible to the poor (*ibid.*).

In fact the above approaches could be summed up as provision of an enabling environment for the poor in order to help them house themselves. Governments therefore should design strategies that empower the poor to construct their own house. In addition to creating an enabling environment, however, a strategy that focuses on availing rental houses should be considered. There is also a need to make co-habitation possible. These strategies would increase access to housing for both residential and home-based activities.

Social Capital

Social capital is now understood as an important strand of urban poverty reduction (Phillips 2002). The relationships and networks developed and drawn upon by the urban poor to survive and improve their livelihood are recognized as vital parts of the livelihood strategies (*ibid.*). Social capital in the form of neighbourhood association, though to a varying degree across towns, was found to be high among the urban poor in the present study. Neighbourhood associations and support from neighbours are found to be more important in Addis Ababa and small towns than in the big towns. Similarly, neighbourhood connection was found to be useful in increasing access to services and providing information. This suggests that social capital does play a role in the economic wellbeing of poor households. If neighbourhood associations are critical and important, there is then a need to strengthen such associations. Policies and projects that build or contribute to existing networks in urban areas are needed. This involves understanding a range of social and economic factors influencing social capital in urban areas. Power relationships in terms of who controls resources and authority, the mobility of the poor, government laws and policies and other processes influencing social capital need to be understood (*ibid.*).

6.1.2 Income Earning Activities

The income dimension remains an important aspect of poverty despite criticisms that it represents a narrower definition of poverty (Amis 2002). For example, in the Indian slum improvement project, it has been found that half the statements made by the poor households about important factors that lead out of poverty are related to incomes, assets and livelihoods (*ibid.*).

In the FGDs held in this study, a poor person was defined as someone "who is capable of working but is short of money". This understanding of poverty by the community underlies the importance of labour as a major resource of the poor and the importance of income as a means of getting out of poverty.

The stimulation and support of income earning activities are therefore central to poverty reduction and livelihood improvements.

Urban economic growth is very closely related to income dimension of poverty. The state of the economy or the economic health is transmitted to households through mechanisms such as increase or decrease of wage and employment, increase or decrease of cost of living etc (*ibid.*). Economic decline increases poverty while progress has the opposite effects. Mechanisms to stimulate the economy and generate employment will therefore establish strong bases for improving the income conditions of the poor. The following are among such mechanisms.

Local Economic Development

Lack of jobs and investment are considered important causes of poverty in many towns, and particularly in small towns. This was made very explicit in many focus group discussions. In the Asendabo FGD, for example, it was stated that there is no economic activity in the area and this created hostile environment for employment and job creation. In the Wuchale Focus Group, it was mentioned that lack of investment in the town was an important cause for lack of opportunity. It was also pointed out that most people were illiterate and that prevented people from being employed even if there waere jobs. The same idea was raised in Welenchit and Adama FGDs as well. The creation of employment and stimulation of investment by the local government should thus be given high priority.

In this regard, members of the FGDs group discussions were able to articulate the various assistances they require from the government and non-governmental agencies (see Table 6.1). The envisaged activities include provision of immediate relief, reduction of the high cost of living, employment creation, credit, subsidy for children education, provision of urban land, provision of *kebele* house and construction of toilet. Employment creation was one of the interventions mentioned most frequently by the poor.

Table 6.1 Types of support required from the government, by frequency

Support required to improve livelihood	Response Frequency
Immediate relief	Most frequent
Reduction of cost of living	Most frequent
Employment creation	Most frequent
Credit	Most frequent
Food for work	Less frequent
Food aid for the elderly and those with no pension	Less frequent
Educational subsidy	Most frequent
Provision of urban land	Less frequent
Provision of *Kebele* house	
Construction of toilet	Less frequent
Good governance, transparency and just way of doing things	Less frequent

SOURCE: Own survey

Employment creation can be achieved by investment expansion and stimulation of economic development at local level. Local economic development is one important function of urban local governments. It entails the stimulation of the local economy by forging partnership between different actors in the locality. In addition, municipalities can assist local economic development by creating conducive business environment. This can have two dimensions. First is the stimulation of local agglomeration in the form of creating a critical pool of skilled labour supply and knowledge creation. Training, education, and provision of incentives can develop the critical mass of agglomeration to support sustainable development. The second is to support the local economies to respond to competitive challenges through diversification and upgrading of the existing activities (Tegegne 2009).

Enterprise Development

The main asset on which the poor draw on is their labour. This study has confirmed that self-employment is an important part of the livelihood of the poor households in small and big towns. These enterprises are managed mainly by owners alone since they are small in their capacity. In many cases, the businesses are not prospering and show no change. A strategy to promote and support these small enterprises and businesses is therefore very critical to support livelihood. A study in Ghana (Menash, Tribe and Weiss 2007) showed that small enterprises are part of a 'sustainable livelihood strategy' of lowering economic risks by diversifying income sources.

Home- based Enterprises

A home-based enterprise is based on or is very close to home instead of a commercial or industrial building or area. Many low-income households rely on home-based enterprises for employment, income and services. Without-home based enterprises large households would have found it difficult to survive (Tipple 2003).

This study showed that home-based enterprises are very important in Addis Ababa, where 70 per cent of the people running business reported the same. The findings in small towns (29 per cent) and big towns (27 per cent) are comparable to other African studies which reported 20-24 per cent of the poor's activity to be home-based activity (*ibid.*). It is very essential to understand the nature of home-based enterprises in terms of their various requirements and characteristics to design a meaningful strategy. It could, however, be said that since they have important role in the livelihood, they should be given attention by policymakers. In other words, ways of assistance to make them effective and efficient need to be designed. One approach would be to link them with other entrepreneurs and meet their needs for adequate space, water supply, sanitation, power, and the like.

6.1.3 Vulnerability and Coping Mechanisms

Food shortage, ill health, complete loss of income and eviction from houses were the four major events and shocks faced by many households in this study. There were, however, significant differences among towns. Shocks are more of a problem of households in small towns than of big towns.

Some of the respective coping strategies households employ were found to be not sustainable and having possible long-term negative effects. In the FGDs it was stated that "a poor person eats when he only gets something to eat but goes without food if there is nothing to eat". In the household study, it was found out that decreasing food consumption and buying less nutritious, cheap food were some of the coping strategies regardless of their health impact. In view of this, it can be said that urban food security strategies should be designed in order to reduce the households' vulnerability to food shortage.

As ill health is a serious threat to the livelihood of the poor, preventive and curative efforts have to be put in place. Preventive efforts related to improving the conditions of living by increasing access to sanitation, water, and other similar basic necessities should be put in place. Likewise, curative services involving medical treatment should be made accessible to the poor.

Loss of income was reported as the third major shock by households. As stated earlier, the main sources of income for the poor are both casual work and self-employment. Loss of income could thus arise from lack of casual work or business bankruptcy. While efforts to increase job opportunities should be undertaken, it has to be accompanied, however, by safety nets in urban areas. It should be noted that safety nets are widely used in rural Ethiopia. However, similar programmes, are not available in urban areas in order to rescue the vulnerable. Thus it stands to reason that it is imperative to develop safety nets that protect the urban poor and help them mitigate risks.

Eviction from houses is another important shock that need to be dealt with. In this regard, it is imperative to understand the causes of eviction. It seems that inability to pay house rent could lead to eviction. Under such circumstances ways of increasing the income of the poor could go a long way in alleviating the problem. In addition, the housing strategy that aims at creating an enabling environment for the poor to house themselves will help counteract shocks from house eviction. As well, instituting legal systems that protect citizens from random evictions would be a major step forward in tackling the shock in this regard.

6.2 Linkages and Gaps

6.2.1 The MSE Strategy

The major linkage between livelihood requirements outlined above and the existing poverty reduction strategy described in chapter five is the enterprise development or the MSE strategy. The government's MSE approach to alleviate poverty is a step in the right direction. The literature supports the MSE approach to poverty reduction. In fact it is one of the enduring approaches of poverty reduction. The idea emerged in the 1980s as a result of interest in the informal sector. It is a meeting point between the neo-liberal interest to promote private enterprise and the market as creators and distributors of resources and grassroots practitioners' focus on the on-the ground problem of poverty recognizing local people's own agency (Eversole 2004). Micro-enterprise development provides a perfect opportunity for self-help development as poor people in developing countries are observed to create wealth and employ themselves. The approach looks at the poor people as entrepreneurs. As a result, development interventions at various levels embraced micro-enterprises as the key to unlocking the potential of stagnant economies and improving the livelihoods of the poor (ibid.). For example, the World Bank approved more than 10 billion in MSE support between the years 1998-2003, including 1.5 billion in 2003 (Beck et al. 2003).

The core principle in MSE development approach to poverty reduction is that by expanding entrepreneurship, MSEs provide employment and thus sustainable income. They also provide lower level goods and services for the poor people. The profits from MSEs also remain locally, creating flow-on benefits to the disadvantaged areas. Thus the benefits from micro-enterprises accrue to individuals, families and communities.

Despite the MSE policy being in the right direction and there is enough justification for it, the programme seems to be ambitious and complex particularly at its implementation stage. First, the amount of resources estimated for micro-enterprises is huge (6.2 billion birr). It will not be easy to raise this funding. The flow of resources from micro finance will not be also easy since the business of lending requires the fulfilment of credit worthiness and other pre-requisites which may not be easily attainable by operators of MSEs. In fact it is seen that unavailability of loan in some towns is a major difficulty. Second, though goal 7 of the urban development package demands setting aside of 4900 hectares of land for MSEs, the pace of preparing land and its availability varies among cities and towns posing its own challenges. Urban land also has competing uses exacerbating further the challenges to municipalities. Third, the government hopes to deploy extension workers to undertake the programme. This necessitates training at the required level and speed. The result of the programme thus depends on the effectiveness of extension workers which cannot be ensured easily. Fourth, group-based or association-based MSE strategy is a supply side strategy that forces individuals to form groups to qualify for assistance. In many towns, however, lack of interest to form groups and lack of cohesion even among those who formed groups have surfaced. These will jeopardize the association-based model of MSE development. Fifth, in order for MSEs to grow and compete, there is a need to upgrade technologies. Technology upgrading requires continuous training, investment and support and this poses its own pressure on the programme and the government.

Besides implementation problem, the other major problem of the MSE strategy is the secondary status given to existing micro enterprises (as opposed to new start-ups) and lack of attention to develop and promote these enterprises. The existing enterprises are major employers and could have a potential to employ more if they are assisted effectively. It is therefore easier to promote existing enterprises in all cities while also providing space and conducive environment for new start-ups as well. An additional major gap in the MSE strategy is its neglect of home-based activities and enterprises. Home based activities are significant in our study and the literature suggests that the majority of poor people derive livelihood from home-based activities. Support for these activities by linking them with entrepreneurs and providing them with adequate space and housing should have been undertaken as a strategy of poverty reduction.

6.2.2 The Integrated Housing Development Program (IHDP)

As indicated above the IHDP programme has a number of objectives. The provision of employment and low cost housing are the two major objectives that directly affect the urban poor. The employment potential of housing construction is essentially a useful way of poverty alleviation. This is due to the fact that such employment is highly suited to people with limited skills and it can be identified to be self-selecting the poor (Tipple 1999). Small scale enterprises in the housing sector are important in maximizing employment in construction and related sector in four ways. First, they use labour intensive method in the absence of machinery. Second, they use local knowledge and work within local neighbourhood and provide better services based on customers need. Third, they can develop from a very small scale, often the home, and provide jobs for skilled and unskilled persons; Fourth, they can use local inputs with minimum imports (*ibid.*).

The use of shelter to increase employment, however, need to be empirically studied to identify the real poverty and employment impact in terms of technology adopted, earnings, etc. A study on the employment impact of the Addis Ababa integrated housing development programme found that the technology used by the firms in the programme was not different from firms not participating in the programme (Rijekers, Laderichi, and Teal 2008). Programme firms are not more labour intensive and do not use more skilled labour than non-programme firms. Since programme firms have not altered technology and labour intensity, they did no generate higher labour demand than would have been generated had contracts been awarded to existing firms (*ibid.*). In terms of earnings, programme firms have higher earning premiums, but this may reflect the return to capital as workers in programme firms are also owners of the firm (*ibid.*). The evidence therefore is not favourable regarding the labour intensive nature of such ventures.

The provision of low-cost housing for the poor through construction of condominium houses is the second objective of the IHDP programme in alleviating poverty. In this regard, studies have shown that condominium houses could be low-cost but are not low-income houses. Condominium houses are of different sizes. The houses are provided for those who qualify on the basis of a certain upfront payment and long term payment of the balance. In many study towns and cities, it was indicated that there is a need to pay 20 per cent of the total cost as down payment and this amounts to about 16,000 birr on average. This kind of upfront payment is far from the reaches of the poor. The cost of the project is not also within the reach of the poor. In particular houses with bigger rooms are not affordable by the poor who have large family sizes (Yewineshet 2007). Loan arrangements also favour government workers which automatically disqualify the poor who are not working in the government sector (*ibid.*).

As a result, despite the expressed aim of condominium projects to address the needs of the poor, studies have shown that a significant portion of these units are occupied by middle and high-income households. Data from condo sites located in several sectors of Addis (Aware, Gulele, Urael, Lideta, Mekanisa, and Bole-Gerji), showed that over 60 per cent of the occupants are middle and upper income households (Assefa and Tegegene 2008). In the Bole-Gerji site, only 1.3 per cent of condo occupants are low-income households (Seyoum 2007).

6.2.3 Land Delivery

Provision of land, infrastructure, services and facilities is one of the four pillars of the urban development packages. The relation between land delivery and poverty is emphasized in PADSEP. Land delivery is a major housing strategy in both small and big towns.

Land delivery for the poor, however, is fraught with problems. A study revealed that the majority of officials in Ethiopian towns agree that land delivery is ineffective in addressing the needs of the poor people (Gondo 2008). A number of challenges are also forwarded as contributing to the ineffective land delivery to the poor. These include time consuming and flawed procedures, lack of participation of the poor in land delivery, weak monitoring and evaluation system, poor saving capacity and lack of collateral by the poor (*ibid.*).

In towns under this study, it was possible to discern that first, there is a mismatch between demand and supply. The latter is not capable of coping with the former as land preparation and allocation lags behind the land demand. This is evidenced by long waiting list for extended period of time in many towns. Second, land delivery, particularly the lottery allocation, is based on upfront payment and long term payment. The upfront payments in the small towns range from 400 to 2500 birr while in big towns it goes to as high as 4000 birr. These are not easily affordable by the poor.

When poor city inhabitants get land by lottery without the ability to make the required payments, they are likely to "sell" their winnings over to others who have the financial means to secure tenure for their own use or to speculate for subsequent transfer (Assefa and Tegegne 2008).

6.2.4 Livelihood Issues not Addressed by Poverty Reduction Strategies

Several livelihood requirements are not addressed by the existing urban poverty reduction policies. These include:

a) Asset building strategies: There are no major asset building strategies targeted towards the urban poor. The deficiencies of the urban poor in human and financial capital are noted above. Any effort of poverty alleviation will not be sustainable if deficiencies in these key assets are not overcome. Strategies which aim at enhancing both contribute towards improved livelihood; and

b) Coping mechanisms and vulnerabilities: Food security programmes and safety net programmes are not part of the urban poverty reduction strategies. These strategies however are in dire need in the face of food shortage the urban poor face and the loss of income they encounter. Unless attended, lack of food and lack of income are basically the major ingredient that deteriorate people's livelihood.

6.2.5 Urban Policy Based on Similarities and Differences

The type of urban policy to be formulated should be based on issues that consider the differences and similarity among a spectrum of towns. The current policy prescribes similar range of policy for all towns. This assumes the nature of urban poverty is similar in all towns. Households, however, face different asset status and undertake different livelihood strategies across a range of towns. The prescribed uniform policy will not be able to address the different needs of the poor in different settings. For example, in this study it was shown that housing is a major problem of big cities and Addis Ababa while lack of human capital is severe among the poor in small towns. Similarly, the poor in small towns are better off in terms of physical assets such as livestock ownership and housing stock. These assets could be considered as strength of the poor in small towns and it is possible to build on them. On the other hand, similarity among households such as reliance on neighbourhood association, lack of saving and credit, skill deficiency could be used to forge similar policies across the towns.

6.2.6. Urban Governance and Poverty Reduction

Urban governance includes broad range of actors: the private sector, NGOs, community organizations, religious groups, trade unions and trade associations, central and local government. The focus on this paper is on urban governments namely the city governments in big towns and municipalities in small towns which are the main providers of services that affect the poor. It is, however, possible to make note of some elements of governance as it affects poverty.

Devas (2001) mentions that there are three broad areas in which the link between urban governance and poverty can be made. These are 1) the political process and whether this enables the voices of the poor to be heard; 2) the capacity of the city government to respond to the needs of the poor; and 3) the impact of civil society on access and influence by the poor.

An institutional arrangement and political process that make the votes of the poor count and allow the poor influence decisions which affect them could be designated as a political process that is inclusive of the poor (Devas 2001). In Ethiopia, Council members at city, sub-city, and *kebele* levels are elected on party basis. There is no provision which ensures the representation of the poor in the council. This means that there are no council members elected representing the poor segment of the society. In the absence of the poor in the council, the chances for the interest and causes of the poor to be reflected adequately in decision making is very low. In big cities, including Addis Ababa, the Mayor is elected by fellow Councillors and this is a political decision. In small towns, town mangers are appointed by the *woreda* administration. The Mayor is not obliged to campaign on behalf of the poor residents of the city. Under such circumstances, responsiveness to the interests of the poor will not be a major requirement of the Mayor. *Kebele* level election has more potential to address the needs of the poor since they are close to the population. However, party agenda remains to be the dominant pre-occupation for the election of the *kebele* chairman rather than the agenda of the poor.

The extent to which City Governments, Municipalities and *Kebele* administrations can benefit the poor also depends on their capacity to deliver. There are a number of deficiencies in this regard. First, there is a high level of centralization of activities and decisions at city, municipal level and sub-city level. This is true in all towns. In all city administrations and towns, major decisions are undertaken by the municipality. The *Kebeles* are only implementing arms of the municipality with limited functions, powers and resources. The *Kebeles* are, however, the closest units to city residents and are places to where the poor city residents come for assistance and services. The high level of centralization of decisions at city level will bring not only ineffective excercise of responsibilities but also precludes the desired participation of the people and low level authorities in addressing real problem on the ground. Secondly, city administrations and municipalities invariably have shortage of resources that preclude them from discharging their service provision responsibility. There is a significant mismatch particularly at municipality level between the revenue capacity and the economic and social expenditure need. Both city governments and municipalities also suffer from technical capacity problem. In many cases, the required experts and professionals are not available and this brings lack of vision and failure in accurately understanding the problem and the solution. Thirdly, municipalities in small towns are subordinate to the *Woreda* Government and they do not belong to *woreda* cabinet. They, therefore, have limited decision-making capacity on resources, plans and programmes of the *woreda*. Under such circumstances, municipalities cannot provide adequate services to residents.

The poor can make its voices heard through civil societies (Devas 2001). Civil society place demands on the state for goods and services, promote the broad interest of their constituencies, and extend the social space between the state and the individual (Desallegn 2002). According to Dessalegn (2002) there is a need for formal organization for the existence of the civil society. This means the poor and the dispossessed need to formally organize and legally register as much as the middle class and the professionals. These types of organizations include non-government organizations, advocacy organizations, interest group organizations and community organizations (*ibid.*). Along this line, the urban poor can organize and create interest groups such as associations of casual workers or self-employed people. These kinds of organizations, however, were not evident in the study areas. It therefore seems to be in the interest of the poor to encourage and support such organizations.

Beyond formal organizations, the poor, however, are part of informal organizations such as '*idir*', and neighbourhood associations. This was revealed in this study as evidenced by the contributions the poor make to '*idir*' and the role and importance of neighbourhood associations. These organizations have specific objectives and form bases for neighbourhood solidarity. It is, however, noted that their capacity to transcend their narrow objectives and articulate public demands is very limited (Dessalegn 2002).

As a result, at their present level of development, their capacity to represent the poor and make the voices of the poor heard is low. This begs the need to strengthen the capacities of the informal organizations to make claims and demand services from the government.

6.3 Summary on Livelihood Requirements and Linkages

The assets and livelihood analysis serve as pointers to derive livelihood requirements of the poor. In this study, it has been noted that asset building strategies are those which can easily be derived from the recognition of the fact that the poor are asset-less. Financial, human and social capitals are considered as important assets to be built in urban areas. In addition, the housing shortage and lack of housing point to the importance of enhancing the housing asset. Income earning activities in the forms of local economic development, enterprise development and home based activities also form important requirement of the poor in the study area. The fact that households experience shocks indicates the need and importance of safety nets. This was also emphasized in the Focus Group Discussion.

In terms of linkage with government policy, the MSE strategy and the Housing programme have the potential of addressing the livelihood requirements of income generation and housing asset building. Their adequacy and effectiveness, however, merits further investigation. The numerous problems faced by these strategies could be stumbling blocks. In addition, the issue of targeting and affordability are critical particularly with housing programme.

There are several areas where gaps between policy and livelihood requirements are shown. These include asset building strategies, coping mechanisms, and instituting differentiated strategy across towns and cities instead of their uniform applications.

In terms of urban governance it was highlighted that efforts to ensure the representation of the poor and to strengthen their civil societies are badly needed.

CHAPTER 7
CONCLUSION

The world is increasingly becoming urbanized and with it we have a significant urbanization of poverty. The urban poverty agenda, however, has been neglected in major development discourse (Amis 2001). In Ethiopia, urban development in general and urban poverty in particular has been neglected as policies and programmes focused more on rural poverty and rural development. The explicit mention of urban poverty was made only in the recent PASDEP.

The magnitude of the problem in Ethiopia is quite huge. Not only does a significant proportion of the urban population live in poverty but it shows an increasing trend from time to time. Thus, there is a need to adequately understand the nature of urban poverty in order to devise effective intervention measures. To date, efforts have been made in Ethiopia to measure the incidence, depth and severity of poverty in line with the consumption/income understanding of poverty. These efforts, worthwhile as they are, do not address the livelihood of the poor in terms of the assets the poor possess and the strategies they adopt to run their livelihood. Moreover, the status of the urban poor differs across a spectrum of towns since the poor living in different places face different opportunities and constraints and possess different levels and types of assets. This calls for the need for policies to be based on the livelihood requirements of the poor. By the same token, it is imperative to appreciate the linkages and gaps policies may have with the livelihood requirements of the poor.

7.1 Lessons Learned or Findings

This study had three primary objectives at the outset. The first was to examine the livelihood of the poor in both big and small towns using the livelihood framework. The second one dealt with the identification of the existing policies, and the third was to understand the linkages and gaps of the livelihood framework with the existing urban poverty reduction and governance structure.

With regard to the first objective, the study findings pertain to asset base of the poor, the livelihood strategy, the vulnerability of the poor, along with similarities and differences between small and big towns.

1) In terms of asset base, it has been learnt that the four types of assets, namely physical, human, financial and social capitals, are quite relevant as their presence is reported with varying levels across towns and households. On the other hand, natural asset has not figured prominently in the possession of assets. In sum, however, it has been noted that the urban poor in the study towns are asset poor;

2) In terms of the activities and strategies of the poor, it has been established that the poor participate in income earning activities, social activities, reproductive activities, and undertake consumption cutting strategies. These should be understood as ways and means of pursuing a livelihood given their asset base and status. The major income earning activities, in order of their importance, are casual work, self-employment, and wage employment;

3) Concerning shocks and vulnerabilities, food shortage, loss of income, ill health and eviction from houses were found to be major shocks faced by households. The number of respondents who reported shocks was lower in Addis Ababa than in other places; and

4) With regard to contextual variation in livelihood between small and big urban centres, it has been learned that there is a difference across towns in households' asset possession. Households in small towns are better endowed with livestock resources and house asset. Conversely, households in big towns and Addis Ababa seem to fare better in education level than households in small towns. On the other hand, there is a similarity across all households in all cities and towns with regard to their financial capital and skill levels. Accordingly, savings and access to credit are, by and large, low for all households. Skill deficiency was also reported to be low to a similar extent among all households in different towns. On the positive side, reliance on neighbourhood associations as a form of social capital is observed across households in all towns. Similarly, poor households in all towns possess many adult people which could be potential labour force to generate income. The livelihood strategies across a range of towns showed little or no difference. These activities yield low and irregular income, thereby exposing the poor to shocks and vulnerabilities.

With regard to the second objective, the study has revealed that the Urban Poverty Reduction Strategy in Ethiopia is a national strategy that focuses on MSEs and housing developments. These are pertinent policies and programmes that are commonly applied in all the study cities and towns. These policies and programmes, however, show implementation problems related to shortages of inputs, such as land and capital, and problems of targeting and organisation. Moreover, the new urban governance recognizes municipalities, city administrations and sub-cities. These entities are given authority, responsibility and resources. Capacity constraint and resource deficiency, however, are noted in several places.

In relation to the third objective, this study has found some linkages and gaps between the existing poverty reduction strategy and the actual livelihood requirements. The linkages between the livelihood requirements and policies are in connection with employment and housing needs of the poor. Income earning activities are one of the livelihood requirements of the poor. The income of the poor could be improved through promoting employment in small enterprises, stimulating the whole economy and assisting the activities in which the poor are engaged. The MSE strategy of the government has the main objectives of creating employment and improving income. This then clearly shows the linkage between the livelihood needs of the poor and the government policy. The housing policy with its twin objectives of increasing housing for the poor and stimulating micro enterprises is closely related with the needs of the poor for house asset and employment. The gaps are mainly in relation to the asset needs, vulnerabilities, and home-based activities of the poor. These issues, however, are not addressed in the current urban poverty reduction strategies.

7.2 Implications of the Study Findings

This study has theoretical, policy and research implications.

Theoretical Implications

The theoretical implications of the study pertain to the application of the livelihood strategy in urban setting. The application of the livelihood framework in urban setting is not widely practiced in the literature. This study has demonstrated that the prediction of the livelihood framework that the poor are engaged in multidimensional activities is true in urban setting of a developing country. The application of the livelihood framework in urban setting, however, requires that some urban features be given emphasis in comparison to the rural application. Some of these urban features, as indicated in the literature, include sources of vulnerability, the importance of income from sale of labour, the role of domestic services, urban agriculture, house renting, access to credit, house possession and urban systems of governance in the livelihood of the urban poor.

The importance of some of these features has come out very clearly in this study. For instance, the role of housing and income from sale of labour has been highlighted in this study. Urban agriculture and access to credit, however, have not figured prominently in the total sample of the study. Similarly, the role of urban systems of governance in addressing poverty reduction was less significant in this study. The *Kebeles* which are the closest institutions to the poor have no capacity and the authority to address the poverty situations.

A very significant theoretical implication of the study is that the livelihood of the poor show differences and similarities between big cities and small towns. The difference is more pronounced in asset possession. The poor in different towns are not similarly endowed with the four capitals – physical, social, financial, and human. The endowment of some capitals is associated with the ease of access to these capitals. For example, access to land is easier in small towns than in bigger towns. As a result, a higher proportion of the poor have better possession of house than those in big towns. Similarly, access to education is easier in big towns than in small towns. As a result a higher proportion of the poor in big towns have better human capital. It is therefore important to specify the contextual setting when discussing the livelihood of the poor in an urban setting.

Policy Implication

The main purpose of the Poverty Reduction Strategy and policy is to reduce the level of poverty among the poor. It has been clearly stated above that the government has some urban poverty reduction policies put in place though they are fraught with implementation problems. These policies could be used as stepping stones to further poverty reduction efforts and improve the livelihood of the poor. While the specific policies of MSE development and Housing strategies need to be continued by overcoming their weaknesses, there are other policy measures that need to be focused on too. These are:

i.) *Asset Building Strategies*: The study has established that, though assets are the bases on which the livelihood of the poor depends, the poor in general are asset-less. This implies that the government should strive to improve the asset endowment of the poor. This applies to all kinds of assets, including financial, human, physical and social. The provision of training to improve the human capital of the poor and thereby improve their employability needs to be the focus of the policy. Similarly, the poor should have easy access to credit in order to improve their financial status;

ii.) *Local Economic Development*: Lack of investment and economic decline of cities, particularly in small towns, has been noted in the study. A wider stimulation of the economic activity or initiatives for local economic development are therefore needed to enhance the absorbing capacities of towns and cities;

iii.) *Home-based Activities and Casual Activities*: The study has confirmed that home-based activities are activities in which the poor are engaged. Thus, they need to be promoted in order to address the needs of the poor under the MSE strategy. The poor in general derive income from casual activities. There is therefore a need to support these causal activities as long as they are socially acceptable income earning activities;

iv.) *Improving the Housing Condition and its Affordability*: This study showed that, though some of the poor possess houses, the quality of their houses is very deplorable. Rented houses, which are mostly *kebele* owned, are also in the same deplorable conditions. This is one source of vulnerability. The unaffordability of the housing programme for the poor was also established in this study, and this is an indication that the poor are being bypassed as far as their needs for shelter is concerned. As housing is an important asset of the poor in urban setting, improving the housing condition of the poor and increasing the affordability of the housing programmes needs to pursued;

v.) *Poverty Reduction Policies Should be Differentiated*: This study has shown existing variations among towns in the livelihood endowment of the poor. It is therefore a short step to think in terms of differentiated urban poverty reduction policies. These include, among others, strengthening education in small towns since low levels of education is observed in small towns and alleviating housing problem in big cities since this is a major concern of the poor in big cities. Similarly, one could capitalize on opportunities such as urban agriculture and livestock endowment in small towns;

vi.) *Urban Safety Nets*: The fact that the poor face different shocks, such as food shortage, ill health, and house eviction, signify that the poor are always vulnerable to changes in their life time, endowment and external situations. There is a need to institute urban safety net programmes that address such vulnerabilities and help the poor cope with shocks; and lastly

vii.) *Strengthening City-level Institutional Capacity*: Capacity gaps in different towns whether related to resources, manpower, or lack of devolution, constrain the role of city-level institutions in addressing the problems of poverty. The institutions follow a nationally designed policy and strategy and there is little innovation and initiation to deviate from such policy and design an appropriate context-specific policy of their own. The participation of the poor in decision making is wanting because institutions at city level are organized on the basis of party allegiances. Under such circumstances, it is not clear how the agenda of the poor filters into *kebele* and city level authorities. On the beneficiary side, the absence of an organization that can articulate the demand of the poor and put pressure on the government adds to institutional deficiency. It is therefore crucial that the institutional deficiency observed at municipal and *kebele* levels, and even at the level of the beneficiaries, be rectified and appropriate mechanisms designed for such endeavour.

Suggestions for Future Research

There are several aspects of the study which point out the need for further research. Among these are:

a. The poor in general derive income from casual activities. There is a need to understand what these casual activities are, how much they pay, and what is the condition of their work and why the poor find themselves in these activities. It will also be interesting to find out what are the specific characteristics of the poor who are mostly engaged in casual activities as opposed to those who are engaged in self employment or wage labour;

b. This study has found that credit, an important financial resource, does not figure prominently in the livelihood of the poor. It will be interesting to identify the real cause of such low reliance on credit by the poor to enhance their livelihood. Some of the possible reasons that go towards explaining the phenomenon but which require investigations are lack of sufficient institutional mechanisms to provide credit for the poor, the capacity of the poor to take loan, the attitude of the poor towards credit, and the like;

c. Skill deficiency is noted among all households in the study. It is clearly known that skill deficiency affects the employability of the poor negatively. This implies that there is a need to improve the skill endowment of the poor., However, further research is needed to identify the types of skill needed by whom and where. Similarly, it will also be important to identify the different modalities and duration of delivering skill for the poor so that effective results could be obtained; and finally

d. The existing urban poverty reduction strategies and policies have specific goals and objectives. The policies have identified beneficiary or target groups, mechanisms of implementation and inputs. The extent to which these policies have brought changes in the livelihood of the poor, however, is not known. It will be useful to study their impacts on the beneficiaries of the programme.

Endnotes

1. A '*kebele*' (Amharic term) is the smallest local government unit in urban areas. Its official name is urban dwellers association and it has a defined geographic area.

2. This section draws heavily from Farrington *et al.* (2002)

3. The three towns, namely Addis Ababa, Jimma, and Adama are the towns selected for this study

4. There is a discrepancy of 2 between those who reported house possession and those who reported to live in their own houses. The discrepancy between the two for small towns is 3, 2 for big towns, and 1 for A.A. Since the two questions were asked separately, the discrepancy could have been the result of misunderstanding the questions.

5. A type of baking pan used for preparing "Injera', a traditional food in Ethiopia

6. '*Equib*' is an Amharic term which means traditional rotating saving scheme in which people voluntarily engage in.

7. The *chi-square* value was found to be 4.4. for 2 degrees of freedom. The tabulated value for the same degrees of freedom at 95 level of confidence is 5.9, forcing us to accept the null hypothesis that there is no difference among the towns.

8. The calculated *chi-square* value is 25.78 with df of 2. The tabulated value for 95 level of significance and 2 df is 5.991.

9. 'Injera' is a local food that is made at home.

10. Six of these are in small towns, nine in big towns, and four in A.A. The mean number of hired workers is 3 in small towns, 2.6 in big towns, and 2.2 in A.A.

11. Thirteen of the individuals are in small towns, five in big towns, and four in Addis Ababa. The mean number of family workers are 1.5 in small towns, 1.6 in big towns, and 2.5 in Addis Ababa

12. There is discrepancy between livestock possession reported in Table 4.1 and the livestock possession reported in this section. In this section households were asked about livestock possession from which they generate income. The total number here is 37 households as opposed to 50 households in Table 4.1

13. The mean household sizes were 3.7, 4.2 and 4.9 for urban Amhara, urban Oromiya, and A.A respectively in 2004/05 (WMS 2004/05)

14. In the Ethiopian case, micro enterprises are defined as those with capital amount of less than 20,000 birr, and small enterprises are defined as those with a capital amount of less than 500,000 birr.

15. In Merawi it was established in 2004, in Asendabo it was established in 2007, in Welechiti in 2003, and in Wuchale in 2004.

16. In Bahir Dar the objective of MSE strategy is to create employment for 54,962 unemployed people.

17. Prior to this, municipalities were administered on the basis of obsolete legislation.

18. The other region which has attempted to recognize the role and autonomy of municipalities is the Tigray region.

19. The urban services under the mandates of the office of city service include promotion of micro and small enterprises and industrial services, road construction, road lights, drainage and sewage, traffic density, recreation centres, fire protection, graveyards, supply of land, document authentication and registration service, construction license, promotion of micro and small enterprises, and industrial services.

20. At the time of this study, Jimma did not have town council. It, however, had a Development aAdvisory Committee which is responsible for providing advice and assistance on various development issues of the town.

21. In Welenchit the *woreda* though pays compensation for people displaced during city expansion work.

REFERENCES

Abbi, M. Kedir. 2005. Understanding urban chronic poverty: Crossing the qualitative and quantitative divide. University of Leicester, Department of economics, *CPRC Working Paper* 53.

Addis Ababa City Government. 2002. Addis Ababa in action: City Development Plan 2001-2010 excutive summary. Addis Ababa: City Government.

Addis Ababa City Administration (2009) City government structure. http://www.addisababa.gov.et

Addis Ketema Sub-City.2009. Business processing re-engineering (BPR) study of micro and small enterprises, Addis Ababa, Unpublished (Amharic version).

Akalu Wolde Michael. 1967. Some thoughts in the process of urbanization in the 20th century in Ethiopia. *The Geographical Journal,* no.5, ?

Alazar Amare. 2008. Effectiveness of public service delivery reform implementation in Bahir Dar City Administration. Unpublished Master's thesis, Department of Public Administration and Development Management, Addis Ababa University.

Amis, P. 2001. Attacking poverty: But what happened to urban poverty?. *Journal of International Development* no.13, 353-60.

_____. 2002. Municipal government, urban economic growth and poverty reduction-Identifying the transmission mechanisms between growth and poverty. In *Urban livelihood: A people cantered approach*, edited by A. Rakodi Carole and Lloyd-Jones. London: Earthscan.

Amis, P. and Rakodi, C. 1994. Urban poverty: Issues for research and policy. *Journal of International Development* vol.6, no.5: 627-634.

Assefa Mehretu and Tegegne Gebre-Egziabher. 2008. Marginality, erasure, and intractability in the hyper -nflated urban housing market in Addis Ababa. (forthcoming)

Beall, Jo. 1997. Assessing and responding to urban poverty: Lessons from Pakistan. *IDS Bulletin* 28, no. 2: 58-67.

Beall, Jo. 2002. Living in the past, investing in the future-household security among the urban poor. In *Urban livelihood: A people-centred approach*, edited by A. Rakodi Carole and Lloyd-Jones. London: Earthscan.

Beall, Jo. Crankshaw and Parnell, Susan. 2000. The causes of unemployment in post apartheid Johannesburg and the livelihood strategies of the poor. *Tijdschrift voor Economische en Sociale Geogrfie* 19, no.4: 379-96.

Beall, Jo and Fox, Sean. 2006. Urban poverty and development in the 21st century: Towards an inclusive and sustainable. world. www.oxfam.org.uk/resources/policy/trade/downloads/resarch urban poverty.pdf (accessed on).

Beard, V. A. 2001. Rethinking urban poverty: A look inside the Indonesian households. *Third World Planning Review* 22, no 4: 1-17.

Bebbington, A. 1999. Capitals and capabilities: A framework for analyzing peasant viability, rural livelihood and poverty. *World Development* 27, no.12: 2021-44.

Beck, Thoresten *et al.* 2003. Small and medium enterprise: Growth and poverty: Cross country evidence. World Bank Policy Research Working Paper, 3178.

Bigsten, A. *et al.* 2003. Growth and poverty reduction in Ethiopia: Evidence from household panel survey. *World Development* 31, no 1: 87-106

Birdsall, Nancy and Londono, J. Luis. 1997. Asset inequality matters: An assessment of the World Bank approach to poverty reduction. *American Economic Review*, 87, no.2: 32-37.

Brockerhoff, Martin and Brennan, Ellen. 1998. The poverty of cities in developing regions. *Population and Development Review* 24, no. 1: 75-110.

Carney, D. 1998. Implementing the sustainable rural livelihoods approach. In *Sustainable rural livelihoods: What contributions can we make?* Edited by Carney, D., London: Department for International Development.

Central Statistical Agency (CSA). 2006. Report on the 2005 national labour force survey. *Statistical Bulletin*, no 365, Addis Ababa.

_____. 2007. Statistical abstract. Addis Ababa.

Chambers, Roberts.1995. Poverty and livelihood: whose reality counts? *Environment and Urbanization* 7, no.1: 173-204.

Chambers, R. and R. Conway. 1992. Sustainable rural livelihoods: Practical concepts for the 21st century. *IDS Discussion Paper*, no. 296.

De Haan, Arjan. 1997. Urban poverty and its alleviation: An introduction. *IDS Bulletin* 28, no. 2: 1-8.

De Haan, Leo and Zoomers, Annelies. 2005. Exploring the frontiers of livelihood research. *Development and Change* 36, no.1:27-47.

Dessalegn Rhamato. 2002. Civil society organizations in Ethiopia. In *Ethiopia: The challenge of democracy,* edited by Bahru Zewdie and Pausewang Siegfied. Stockholm :Elanders Gotab.

Dessalegn Rahmato and Aklilu Kindanu. 2002. Livelihood security among urban households in Ethiopia. *FSS Discussion Paper*, no.8.

Devas, N. 2001. The connection between urban governance and poverty. *Journal of International Development* 13 : 989-96.

Dierig, Sandra.1999. *Urban environmental management in Addis Ababa: Problems, policies, perspectives and the role of NGOs.* Hamburg: Institute of African Affairs.

Dubey, Amaresh. *et al.*2001. Occupational structure and incidence of poverty in Indian towns of different sizes. *Review of Development Economics* 5, no 1: 49-59.

Elbers, Willem. 2002. Poverty reduction (be)for(e) profit?: A study about the contribution of the ORET-programme to poverty reduction. Centre for International Development Issues, Nijmegen, *Occasional Paper* no 110.

Ellis, Frank. 2000. *Rural livelihoods and diversity in developing countries.* Oxford: Oxford University Press.

Ellis, Frank and Tassew Woldemariam.2005. Ethiopian participatory poverty assessment, 2004/05, http://siteresources.worldbank.org/INETHIOPIA/Resources/ppa_ethiopia.pdf accessed on 1 September 2006.

Ethiopian Economic Association (EEA). 2004/05. Report on the Ethiopian economy, Addis Ababa, Ethiopia.

Eversole, Robyn. 2004. Solving poverty for yourself: Micro enterprise development microfinance and migration. Available at ww.crsi.mq.edu.au/documents/mobile...rigid.../eversole.pdf

Farrington, John *et al.* 2002. Sustainable livelihood approaches in urban areas: General lessons, with illustration from the Indian Cases Overseas Development Institute. *Working Paper* 162.

Federal Urban Planning Institute (FUPI) and Bahir Dar Metropolitan City Administration (BMCI). 2006. Bahr Dar Integrated Development Plan. Unpublished manuscript Bahir Dar.

Gibert, Alan. 1997. Poverty, regional convergence and development: What kind of relationship. In *Locality, state and development. Essays in honor of Jos G.M Hilhorst* edited by Bert Helmsing and Joe Guimaraes, The Hague: Institute of Social Studies.

Harvie, C. 2003. The contribution of microenterprises to economic recovery and poverty alleviation. in East Asia. Available at http//www.uou.edu.au/commerce/econ//wplist/.html

Hoffman, *et al* .1991. Rental housing in urban Indonesia. *Habitat International* 15: 181-206.

Golini, A. *et al* 2001. Migration and urbanization in Ethiopia with special reference to Addis Ababa, CSA, A.A.

Gondo, Tendayi. 2008. Ethiopia's land delivery system and the poverty challenge: Issues, challenges and prognosis. *Local Governance and Development* 2, no.2: 47-60.

Kakwani, Nanak and Son, Hyun. H. 2006. Pro-poor growth: The Asian experience. UNU-WIDER, Research paper No 2006/56. Available at www.wider.unu.edu.stc/repcc/pdfs/rp2006-56.pdf

Kanbur, Ravi and Squire, Lyn. 1999. The evolution of thinking about poverty: Exploring the interactions. http://unstats.un.org/unsd/methods/poverty/evolution-of-thinking-about-poverty Kanbur sept 1999.pdf

Klasen, S. 2002. In search of the Holy Grail: How to achieve pro-poor growth. http:// ideas.respec.org/p/got/iaidps/096.html

Kronlid, Karin. 2001. Household welfare and education in urban Ethiopia. World Institute for Development Economics Research. *Discussion Paper* no 2001/144.

Lipton, M. and Ravallion, M.1995. Poverty and policy. In *Handbook of development economics,* edited by Behrman, J and Srinavasan. Amserdam: Elsevier Science.

Mabogunje, Akin L.2006. Global urban poverty research agenda: The African case. http://www.wilsoncenter.org/events/docs/Mabogunje

Maxwell, D.2000. Urban livelihoods and food and nutrition security in Greater Ghana, Accra Research Report of IFPRI, No 112.

Meikle, Sheilah. 2002. The urban context and the poor. In *urban livelihoods: A people-centred approach to reducing poverty*, edited by Rakodi Carole and Lloyd-Jones Tony. London: Earthscan.

Mekonen Tadesse.1996. Food consumption and poverty in urban Ethiopia. In *urban livelihoods: A people-centred approach to reducing poverty,* edited by Bereket Kebede and Mekonen Tadesse, A.A.

Mekonen Taddese.1999. Determinants and dynamics of urban poverty in Ethiopia. *Ethiopian Journal of Economics* 8, no.1: 1-20.

Menashi, J.V, Tribe, Michael, and Weiss, John. 2007. The small scale manufacturing sector in Ghana: A source of dynamism or of subsistence income? *Journal of International Development* 19: 253-273.

Mills, E.S and Pernia, Ernesto, M.1994. Introduction and overview. In *Urban poverty in Asia: A survey of critical issues,* edited by Pernia E.M., Hong Kong: Oxford University Press.

Ministry of Finance and Economic Development (MoFED). 2006. A Plan for Accelerated and Sustained Development to End Poverty (PASDEP), Volume I, main text. Available at http://www.mofaed.org/macro/PASDEP 20Final 20English.pdf

_____.2008. Ethiopia: Dynamics of growth and poverty reduction during the last decade (1995/96-2004). Unpublished manuscript.

Ministry of Water Resources (MoWR). 2008. Water sector development (PASDEP), 2007-08 budget year implementation report, Addis Ababa. (Amharic version). Available at http://www.mowr.gov.et

Ministry of Works and Urban Development (MoWUD). 2007. Plan for Accelerated and Sustainable Development to End Poverty (2005-06-2009/10), Plan for Urban Development and Urban Good Governance. Unpublished.

_____. 2008. Integrated Housing Development Programme of the Federal Republic of Ethiopia. Paper presented at the African Ministerial Conference on Housing and Urban Development, Abuja, Nigeria. Unpublished.

Moser, C. 1998. The asset vulnerability framework: Reassessing urban poverty reduction. *World Development* 26, no 1: 1-19.

Moser, Caroline, O.N. 1996. Confronting crisis: A summary of household responses to poverty and vulnerability in four poor urban communities. *Environmentally Sustainable Development Studies and Monograph Series*, no 7, The World Bank, Washington: The World Bank.

Muzzine, Elisa.2008. Urban poverty in Ethiopia: A multifaceted and spatial perspective. The World Bank, Washington, D.C.: The World Bank.

Organization for Economic Co-operation and Development (OECD). 2001. The DAC guidelines for poverty reduction. Paris: OECD publication service Oidhiambo, and Manda.2003. Urban poverty and labour force participation in Kenya. A paper submitted to World Bank Research Symposium, Washington, D.C.

Oromiya Regional Government. 2003. Urban local government proclamation no 65/2003.

Oromiya Urban Planning Institute. 2008. Urban finance of Jimma city, draft report.

Owuor, Samuel Ouma. 2006. Bridging the urban-rural divide: Multi-spatial livelihood in Nakuru town, Kenya. African Studies Centre, *Research Report,* 81.

Payne, Geoffrey.2002 Tenure and shelter in urban livelihoods. In *Urban livelihoods: A people-centred approach to reducing poverty*. Edited by Rakodi, Carole and Lloyd-Jones, Tony. London: Earthscan.

Phillips, Sue. 2002 Social capital, local networks and community development. In *Urban livelihoods: A people centred approach to reducing poverty* edited by Rakodi, Carole and Lloyd-Jones, Tony. London: Earthscan.

Rakodi, A.C. 1995. Rental tenure in the cities of developing countries. *Urban Studies* 32, no4-5: 791-811.

_____. 2002a. A livelihood approach-conceptual issues and definition. In *Urban livelihoods: A people-centred approach to reducing poverty*. Edited by Rakodi, Carole and Lloyd-Jones, Tony. London: Earthscan.

_____. 2002b. Economic development, urbanization and poverty. In *Urban livelihoods: A people centred approach to reducing poverty*. Edited by Rakodi Carole and Lloyd-Jones Tony. London: Earthscan,

Rijekers, Bob, Laderichi, C.R and Teal, Francis. 2008. Who benefits from promoting small and medium scale enterprises: Some empirical evidence from Ethiopia. *Policy Research working Paper*, no. 4629, The World Bank.

Rogerson, C.M. 1996. Urban poverty and the informal economy in South Africa's economic heartland. *Environment and Urbanization*, 18, no.1: 167-179.

Rossieter, Jonny. 2000. Integrated urban housing development. *Working Paper* 1, Available at: www.practicaletion.org/?id=iuhd_working papers.

Rutherford, Stuart; Harper, M. and Grierson, John.2002. Support for livelihood strategies. In *Urban livelihoods: A people-centred approach to reducing poverty,* edited by Rakodi, Carole and Lloyd-Jones, Tony. London: Earthscan.

Sackey, H. A. 2005. .Poverty in Ghana from an asset based perspective: An application of probit technique. African Development Bank.

Satterthwaite, David. 1997 Urban poverty: Reconsidering its scale and nature. *IDS Bulletin* 28, No. 2: 9-23.

_____. 2001 The key issues and the works included. In *Sustainable cities, e*dited by David Satterthwaite. London: Earthscan.

Satterthwaite, David and Tacoli, C. 2002. Seeking an understanding of poverty that recognizes rural-urban differences and rural-urban linkages. In *Urban livelihoods: A people-centred approach to reducing poverty,* edited by Rakodi, Carole and Lloyd-Jones, Tony. London: Earthscan.

Schutte, Stefan. 2004. Urban vulnerability in Afghanistan: Case studies from three cities. Available at: http:// Econpapers.repec.org/paper/agsareucs/14632.htm

Schulpen, L and Gibbon, P.2002. Private sector development, policies, practices and Problems. *World Development* 30:1-15.

Seyoum Abadi. 2007. Assessment on the socio-economic composition of condominium housing: Residents and views towards the quality of their buildings in Addis Ababa. Unpublished MA thesis, Addis Ababa: Regional and Local Development Studies, Addis Ababa University.

Shewaye Tesfaye. 2002. A review of institutional capacities to address urban poverty in Ethiopia. In *Poverty and Poverty policy in Ethiopia,* edited by Meret Ayenew, FSS, Addis Ababa

Tacoli, Cecilia. 1999. Understanding the opportunities and constraints for low-income group in the peri-urban interface: the contribution of livelihood frameworks. Development Planning Unit, Strategic Environmental Planning and Management for the Peri-urban Interface Research Project.

Tegegne Gebre-Egziabher. 2005. Rural urban linkage in Ethiopia: The need to bridge the divide. In *Issues and challenges of local and regional development,* edited by Tegegne Gebre Egziabher and Meine Peter van Dijk. Proceeding of the Third International Policy Workshop in Regional and Local Development Studies, Addis Ababa.

_____ .2007. Geographically differentiated strategy, urbanization agenda and rural-urban linkage: Emerging regional development strategy in Ethiopia. *Regional Development Dialogue* 28, no 1: 131-150.

_____. 2009. Regional and local development in Ethiopia: Problems, policies and new frontiers. Professorial inaugural lecture, unpublished.

Tegegne Gebre-Egziabher and Assfaw Kumsa. 2002. Institutional setting for local level development planning in Ethiopia: An assessment and a way forward. *Regional Development Studies* 8.

Tegegne Gebre-Egziabher and Kasshun Berhanu. 2004. The role of decentralized governance in building local institutions, diffusing ethnic and national conflicts and alleviating poverty in Ethiopia. *Regional Development Dialogue* 25, no.1.

Tegegne Gebre-Egziabher and Meheret Ayenew. 2010. Micro and small enterprises as vehicles for poverty reduction, employment creation and business development: The Ethiopian experience, *FSS Research Report* (forthcoming).

Tesfaye Alemayehu. 2006. The analysis of urban poverty in Ethiopia. http://zeus.econ.umd.edu/cgi-   bin/conference /download.cgi?db_name=ACE2004 & paper_id=168#

Tipple, Graham A.1999. Urban poverty alleviation and housing creation In Urban poverty inAfrica: from understanding to alleviation edited by Jones Sue and Nelson Nici . Southampton: Intermediate technology publications.

_____. 2003. The place of home-based enterprises in the informal sector: Evidence from Cochabamba, New Delih, Surabaya and Pretoria.*Urban Studies*, 42, no. 4 611-632.

UN-Habitat. 2002. *Crime in Nairobi: Results of a citywide victim survey.* Nairobi, *Safer Cities Series,* no 4.

_____. 2007. *The state of the world cities 2006/07.* London: Earthscan.

Vanderschueren, F, *et al.* 1996. *Policy programme options for urban poverty reductions. A framework for action at the municipal level.* Washington, D.C: The World Bank.

Wadhva, K.1990. Rental housing in India: compulsion or Choice? In *Rental housing*, edited by UNCHS, Proceedings of an Expert Group Meeting, Nairobi, UNCHS, pp 20-31.

Weglin, A. Emiel 1999. Urban poverty and local actions towards its reduction. *Regional Development Dialogue*, 20, no 1: 20-36.

Wegline, A. Emiel and Borgamn, Karin, M. 1995. Options for municipal intervention in urban poverty alleviation. *Environment and Urbanization* 7, no.2: 131-152.

World Bank. 1990a. *Urban policy and economic development: An agenda for the 1990s.* Washington, DC: The World Bank.

_____. 1990b. *Poverty: World development report 1990.* Oxford: Oxford University Press.

_____. 2000. *Attacking poverty: World development report 2000/2001.* Oxford: Oxford University Press.

_____.2007. The challenges of urbanization in Ethiopia. Draft, unpublished manuscript.

Wratten, Ellen.1995. Conceptualizing urban poverty. *Environment and Urbanization*, 7, no.1: 11-38.

Yeboah, Ian E.A. 2005. Housing the urban poor in twenty-first century sub-SharanAfrica: Policy mismatch and a way forward for Ghana. *Geo Journal* 62: 147-162.

Yewoineshet Meaza Haregewoin. 2007. Integrated housing development programmes for urban poverty alleviation and sustainable urbanization: The case of Addis Ababa. Paper presented at an international conference in Rotterdam.

Appendix 1: List of people interviewed

1. Ato Dita Kurkura Kena, City Manager, Welenchiti town

2. Ato Abedo Ababiya, Head OF Housing Agency, Jimma

3. Ato Ahemed,Ababora Deputy Chairman, Hermata Mentina *Kebele*, Jimma

4. Ato Sultan, Head of Micro Enterprises Agency, Jimma

5. Ato Menberu, Head, Urban Agriculture, Jimma

6. Ato Legese Lemma, City Manager, Jimma

7. Ato Teshome, Town Manager, Asendabo Municipality

8. Ato Sultan, Head, Micro and Small Enterprise Agency, Asendabo

9. Ato Wondiyalew , Head, Housing Agency, Bahir Dar

10. Ato Shimeles, Head of Urban Agriculture, Bahir Dar

11. Ato Tilahun Berihun, Head, Urban Planning and Land Administration, Bahir Dar

12. Ato Tadios, Head , Micro and Small Scale Enterprise Agency, Bahir Dar

13. Ato Yaye Negatu, *Kebele* administrator, Gishe Abay *kebele*, Bahir Dar city

19. Ato Mekonen Fetene, Town Manager, Merawi Municipality

14. Ato Mognaw Walle, Chairman, *kebele* 01 , Merawi

15. Ato Solomon, Deputy Mayor, Dessie city

16. Ato Michael Taffesse, Urban Agriculture, Dessie

17. Head of Urban Land Administration, Dessie city

18. Head, Housing Agency, Dessie city

19. Chairman, *Kebele* 03, Dessie city

20. Town Manager, Wuchale town

21 Chairman, *Kebele* 01, Wuchale

22. Head, Micro and Small Enterprise, Wuchale

23. Deputy Mayor, Adama

24. Head, Micro and Small Enterprise, Adama

25. Head of Adama Housing Agency

26. Ato Abay, Head of Industry Development, Addis Ketema sub-city

27. Ato Walelegne, Team leader of MSE, Addis Ketema sub-city
28. Ato Solomon, Deputy Chairman of keble 13/15, Addis Ketema sub city

About the Author

Tegegne Gebre-Egziabher is a Professor at the Institute of Regional and Local Development Studies and Department of Geography and Environmental Studies at the Addis Ababa University. He obtained his PhD from the Ohio State University in City and Regional Planning. His research interest areas include urban development, regional planning, and decentralization. He has published in areas of urban poverty, regional development, local economic development, decentralization and urban policy.

CPSIA information can be obtained at www.ICGtesting.com
Printed in the USA
LVOW102127260912

300525LV00002B/10/P